TIDYING UP

CLEAN YOUR SH*T NOW

Getting Things Done Effortlessly Through The Simple Art of Home Organising

TREY WOODS

Copyright © 2020 Trey Woods

All Rights Reserved

Copyright 2020 By Trey Woods - All rights reserved.

The following book is produced below with the goal of providing information that is as accurate and reliable as possible. Regardless, purchasing this eBook can be seen as consent to the fact that both the publisher and the author of this book are in no way experts on the topics discussed within and that any recommendations or suggestions that are made herein are for entertainment purposes only. Professionals should be consulted as needed prior to undertaking any of the action endorsed herein.

This declaration is deemed fair and valid by both the American Bar Association and the Committee of Publishers Association and is legally binding throughout the United States.

Furthermore, the transmission, duplication or reproduction of any of the following work including specific information will be considered an illegal act irrespective of if it is done electronically or in print. This extends to creating a secondary or tertiary copy of the work or a recorded copy and is only allowed with express written consent from the Publisher. All additional right reserved.

The information in the following pages is broadly considered to be a truthful and accurate account of facts and as such any inattention, use or misuse of the information in question by the reader will render any resulting actions solely under their purview. There are no scenarios in which the publisher or the original author of this work can be in any fashion deemed liable for any hardship or damages that may befall them after undertaking information described herein.

Additionally, the information in the following pages is intended only for informational purposes and should thus be thought of as universal. As befitting its nature, it is presented without assurance regarding its prolonged validity or interim quality. Trademarks that are mentioned are done without written consent and can in no way be considered an endorsement from the trademark holder.

Table of Contents

PART I 13

Chapter 1: The Clutter in Your Life 14

  Why You Have Clutter 15

    You Don't Recognize What Clutter Is 15

    You Don't Know How Long You Should Keep Something 16

    You Don't Know How to Store Things 16

    You Are Not Using Clutter Busters 17

    Buying Too Many Things, You Don't Need 17

    You Can't Let Things Go 18

  Endowment Effect 18

  The Consequences of Too Much Clutter 19

    Your Stress Levels Increase 20

    Your Diet Is Impacted in A Negative Way 20

    You Can Develop More Respiratory Issues 20

    Your Safety Is Threatened 21

    Your Love Life Is Jeopardized 21

    Your Kids Will Be Upset 22

    You Will Become Isolated 22

    You Will Miss Out On Getting Promoted 22

    You Are More Likely to Miss Work 23

    Your Productivity Decreases 23

    You Will Develop Poor Spending Habits 24

    You Can Go into Debt 24

  Clutter is Not Just Physical 25

Chapter 2: Breaking Your Relationship With "Stuff" 27

Getting Over the Endowment Effect 27

More Decluttering Tips 28

Stop Buying Stuff You Don't Need 30

The Benefits Of Decluttering 33

Decluttering Equals Increased Focus and Productivity 34

Decluttering and Improved Health 35

   Improved Healthy Habits 35

   Better Self-Care 36

   Losing Weight 36

   Easier to Relax 37

Having More Space 37

6-Week Decluttering Challenge 38

PART II 41

Chapter 1: What is Holding You Back 42

Why People Procrastinate 42

   Abstract Goals 44

   Not Having Foreseeable Rewards 45

   A Disconnect from Our Future Selves 45

   Being Too Optimistic 46

   Being Indecisive 47

   Task Aversion 47

   Perfectionism 48

   Self-Handicapping 48

Other Major Reasons for Not Getting Things Done 49

   Not Sure What to do 50

    There is No Deadline or Accountability 50

    Don't See Any Consequences 51

Why Getting Things Done is Critical 51

Chapter 2: It's Time to Get Things Done 54

Overcoming Procrastination 54

    Don't Catastrophize 54

    Focus on Your "Why" 55

    Get Out Your Scheduler 55

    Be Realistic 56

    Break it Down 56

    Stop With the Excuses 57

    Find an Accountability Partner 57

    Optimize Your Environment 57

    Forgive Yourself 58

Mindfulness Meditation Technique 58

    Body Scan Meditation 59

    Sitting Meditation 59

    Walking Meditation 59

    Simple Mindfulness 60

15 Habits of Highly Productive People 60

Chapter 3: Visualizing a Better Future 63

How to Visualize Your Future 63

More Tips for Visualization 64

    Visualize Your New Life 64

    Create a Vision Board 65

    Write Down Your goals 65

    Let Yourself Zone Out 65

Say Your Goals Out Loud..66

Think About What You Want and not What You Don't Want...............66

Life When You Get Things Done..66

A Feeling of Relaxed Control 67

Your Thinking Will Be Stimulated 67

More Organization and Less Clutter 67

Less Time for Worry..68

Chapter 1: Back to the Basics..70

Chapter 2: Unlocking Your True Purpose Through Mindfulness...............74

Re-centering Yourself 74

Giving Your Emotions Space 76

Making Clear Decisions 77

Keeping Yourself Safe 77

Improving Relationships 78

Fostering True Joy..80

Chapter 3: Moving Mindfully in Daily Life 82

Coming to the Present Moment: Daily Guided Mindfulness Meditation With Journaling (Week 1)..82

Coming to the Present Moment: Daily Guided Mindfulness Meditation With Journaling (Week 2)..86

Coming to the Present Moment: Daily Guided Mindfulness Meditation With Journaling (Week 3)..88

Mini Meditation Toolbox: 15 Quick and Easy Meditations to Integrate Mindfulness Into Your Daily Life...91

Mini Meditation Toolbox: 10 Quick and Easy Meditations to Ease Stress, Depression, Addiction, Anxiety, Pain, Distraction, and Loss Using Mindfulness 100

Chapter 1: Self-Care Is the Best Care.. 109

How Does Self-Care Work..110

How Does Self-Care Improve Self-Esteem and Self-Confidence?...........111

Chapter 2: 114

What Does Good Self-Care Look Like? 114

Good Self-Care Practices 114

Taking Responsibility for Your Happiness 114

You Become Assertive With Others 114

You Treat Yourself As You Would a Close Friend 114

You Are Not Afraid to Ask for What You Want 115

Your Life Is Set Around Your Own Values 115

Chapter 3: Demanding Your Own Self-Care 116

Setting Healthy Boundaries 116

Identify and Name Your Limits..116

Stay Tuned Into Your Feelings...117

Don't Be Afraid of Being Direct 117

Give Yourself Permission to Set Boundaries 117

Consider Your Past and Present 118

Be Assertive 118

Start Small 118

Eliminating Toxicity and Not Caring About Losing Friends 119

Don't Expect People to Change 119

Establish and Maintain Boundaries...119

Don't Keep Falling for Crisis Situations...119

Focus on the Solution...120

Accept Your Own Difficulties and Weaknesses....................................120

They Won't Go Easily 120

Choose Your Battles Carefully 121

Surround Yourself With Healthy relationships 121

How to Focus on Self-Care 121
- Pay Attention to Your Sleep 121
- Take Care of Your Gut 122
- Exercise and Physical Activity Is Essential 122
- Consider a Mediterranean Diet 122
- Take a Self-Care Trip 123
- Get Outside 123
- Bring a Pet Into Your Life 123
- Get Yourself Organized 123
- Cook Yourself Meals At Home 123
- Read Regularly 124
- Schedule Your Self-Care Time 124

Chapter 4: How to Be Happy Being Alone 125

Accept Some Alone Time 125
- Do Not Compare Yourself to Others 125
- Step Away From Social Media 125
- Take a Break From Your Phone 126
- Allow Time for Your Mind to Wander 126
- Take Yourself on a Date 126
- Exercise 126
- Take Advantage of the Perks of Being Alone 126
- Find a Creative Outlet 127
- Take Time to Self-Reflect 127
- Make Plans for Your Future 127
- Make Plans for Solo Outings 127

Chapter 1: Self-Esteem and Valuing Yourself 130

How Low Self-Esteem Is Developed 132

The Different Types of Parents 132

Bullying 133

Trauma 135

The Science of Self-Esteem 137

Chapter 2: How You Can Matter to Yourself 139

How to Build Self-Awareness 140

Recognize What Bothers You About Other People 140

Meditate on Your Mind 141

Draw a Timeline of Your Life 142

Identify Your Emotional Kryptonite 142

Travel and Get Out a Little Bit 143

Pick Up a New Skill 143

Clarify Your True Values 143

Chapter 3: Creating a Stronger Self 145

Managing Your Ego 145

Don't Take Things Personally 146

Accepts All of Your Mistakes 146

Stop Being Self-Conscious 146

Realize That Your Ego Will Never Go Away 148

You Are Not the Best 148

Imagine Your Ego as Another Person 148

Stop Bragging 149

Be Grateful for the Little Things 149

Learn to Compliment Others 149

Forgiving People 150

Overcoming Trauma 153

Chapter 4: Changing Our Minds 156

How To Ignore Things 156
    Stop Comparing Yourself To Others 156
    Ignore Societal Pressure 157
    Start Living In The Present Moment..................................158
    Leverage Your Purpose...158
The Mindset Shift 159
Now That Your Self-Esteem is High 160

PART I

Chapter 1: The Clutter in Your Life

You have probably seen many shows on television about how people hoard several different items, either because they love to shop, or they have collected many articles over time and cannot bear to part with them. It gets to the point where their closets and even their entire homes are filled up completely, and it is nearly impossible to move around. You may know people like this in your own life, or perhaps, you are one of these people. If you are reading this book, then I will assume that the clutter in your space is taking over your life.

Especially in Western society, we have a fascination with material possessions of all types. If we like something, we must have it right away. As a result, we end up purchasing so many different items, and we cannot bear to part with them, even if we don't use them anymore. After several years, our living spaces and office spaces are cluttered. This includes places like the kitchen, living room, and restrooms. So many items get collected that they end up getting stored wherever they can.

You might be wondering what the big deal is. So what if I, or anyone else, collects a lot of items? Well, the stuff is yours, and you have every right to do whatever you want with it. However, what I want to address are the psychological issues that result in clutter building up in your life, as well as the effects the same clutter has on your psyche in the long run.

Why You Have Clutter

There are numerous reasons why you have so much clutter in your life. It is not as simple as forgetting to do your Spring cleaning. Even though this could be a part of it, however, there are deeper issues as well that may reflect certain aspects of your personality. This may be more common than you think because some people are able to artfully hide their clutter behind lock doors, where you will not find it unless you dig deep. You may be hiding your own clutter so that it's not visible to you. However, when you open a certain closet, a few drawers in the house, or walk into your garage or basement, and they are filled with items that you never use, then you may have an issue with clutter.

To be fair, it's almost impossible to have no clutter at all. Having a few extra items on your desk, or a drawer with some junk in the house is not a big deal. However, if it starts to cramp your personal space, then you might have a problem. I will go over some of the main reasons why people have clutter in their homes. See which ones you can relate to.

You Don't Recognize What Clutter Is

Many people allow clutter to build up in their homes because they don't recognize what it is. They have a hard time deciphering between what is valuable and what is just taking up space. Some items were once valuable but haven't been used for a long time. Because it can be hard to recognize what clutter is, people have a hard time letting anything go. They will look at something, suspect that it could come in handy down the line, and then never get rid of it.

You Don't Know How Long You Should Keep Something

This is a huge area of confusion in almost any household. How are you supposed to tell how long to keep something? Many people have no concept of when and where to let things go. I am not just talking about tools or appliances here. This can be related to anything. For example, people still have birthday or holiday cards that are decades old. It is nice to look at these cards and conjure up some nice old memories, but how many reminders of the past do you actually need?

You Don't Know How to Store Things

People often do not know how to store things. It might be because they forget, or they do not know where it should go. Suddenly, you will find something hidden in the weirdest section of your house, or worse, not be able to find it when you need it.

Along the same lines, you have no good organizing routine. Perhaps you are not an organized person, in general. This is not an indictment on you personally. Many individuals lack the ability to organize everything in their lives, and this grows worse with the more items they obtain. You can actually declutter for about

15-20 minutes a day for several days straight, and many of your items will disappear.

You Are Not Using Clutter Busters

Clutter busters are items, such as trays, baskets, jars, hooks, or folders, that can be used to place your materials in specialized locations. Yes, you will still have the items in your home, but at least they won't be in your way all the time. Can you imagine having a toilet brush on your coffee table? I certainly hope not.

Buying Too Many Things, You Don't Need

This is probably the most obvious one. How many of us don't buy things we don't need? From aspirational shopping to impulse buying, our homes are filled with things we bought on a whim. Aspirational shopping comes from our interest in actually doing something, only to realize it's not for us. However, we don't take the time to get rid of the items afterward. For example, we might watch a musician playing the guitar and want to be like him. So, we buy a guitar, end up hating it, or get to busy to practice, and then put it in a closet somewhere.

If you genuinely have an interest in learning something, I think it's great. But at least stick to it for a little while to give it a chance. If you end up not liking it, then sell the items or donate them to someone who will use them.

In this last instance, you may know you are a clutter bug, and may not want to be one, but you can't seem to let things go. You have a weird attachment to them and might not know why. This will require a deeper understanding of who you are and why particular items are hard to let go, even if you never use them.

Assess your own situation and determine which of these reasons are causing you to hold onto clutter. It might be a combination of things, which is fine. The important thing is to recognize why the spaces in your life seem so busy when they do not have to be.

Endowment Effect

There is a phenomenon known as the endowment effect, which can also explain why people have a hard time getting rid of things. This is a type of bias that occurs when people overvalue something simply because they own it. It might have been given to them, or they bought it years ago, but would never consider getting it now. However, since they own it, they place a greater worth on it.

This psychological bias has resulted in many people not being able to part with something. They are not even willing to sell it at a fair price, because they feel no one will pay the real value of it. The ironic part is the person with the attachment would never consider buying the article for nearly the same price they are trying to sell it for. For example, if they have a special coffee mug, they will put it on the market for $10, but if they saw the mug in a store, they will not even consider purchasing it. It seems that ownership gives people a certain sense of power, and they hate giving it up.

There is also a concept in psychology known as loss aversion. This is where people feel the pain of losing something at a higher intensity than the joy of gaining something of equal value. For example, if a person loses five dollars, but then finds five dollars somewhere else, the original pain of losing money will still affect them more than the joy of finding money. This can be another reason the endowment effect is so powerful. If a person owns an item, getting rid of it in exchange for the actual value will not be acceptable to them. Therefore, individuals who are impacted by this mindset will overly price something to compensate for their feelings of loss.

The endowment effect is an interesting bias that is still being studied today. It is not completely understood why this mindset affects people. But it definitely does.

The Consequences of Too Much Clutter

While you may think that too much clutter just means you will have a hard time moving around stuff, the consequences actually go much deeper than that. There are numerous negative results that happen due to excess clutter, and some of them might surprise you. After this, you will probably be more motivated to clean up a little bit.

Your Stress Levels Increase

People who live in cluttered environments have higher levels of stress and fatigue. Even increased amounts of the stress hormone, cortisol, was found in their blood. Because individuals stayed in these environments, their cortisol levels never dropped throughout the day, causing chronic stress, more chronic disease risks, and even greater mortality risk.

Your Diet Is Impacted in A Negative Way

Psychological studies have also shown that people who live in more orderly environments tend to choose healthier snack options that those in cluttered areas. Since stress leads to unhealthy snacking, being around too much clutter will lead to poor dietary habits. People also tend to overeat with too much stress.

You Can Develop More Respiratory Issues

Homes that are cluttered tend to attract more dust because there are extra physical items it can settle on top of. Extra dust in the air can eventually lead to respiratory issues in the long run, and can also exacerbate active problems, like asthma or COPD.

The more items you have inside your home, the more dust is generated. This will also attract dust mites. Furthermore, if your clutter gets way too excessive, then several areas of your home will become exceedingly difficult to reach and clean. As a result, more dust will build up. Of course, respiratory issues can lead to even more health consequences.

Your Safety Is Threatened

Too much clutter can lead to an unsafe environment where people can trip and fall easily. You also have more items to bump into when you can't see. In addition, it can be difficult to move around, and essential exits might be blocked. This causes a huge risk if you ever have to evacuate your home urgently. A fire can also spread much more quickly if you have a lot of combustible items lying around.

Your Love Life Is Jeopardized

Clutter can negatively affect marriages, too, as people who have difficulty parting with things may build resentment in their spouse. The clutter does not just impact you, but everyone else in your home too. If the person you love is bothered by the clutter and you're not, then your marriage can definitely suffer.

If you are not married and just dating, imagine what your date would think if she saw your home, and it is completely disorganized. If they don't run for the hills right away, they might do so as soon as the date is over.

Your Kids Will Be Upset

Yes, your kids, who you constantly tell to clean their room, will be upset with excess clutter. Studies have found that kids who live in a cluttered environment tend to have more distress, which will affect other areas of their lives.

You Will Become Isolated

A large number of adults say they won't invite anyone over to their house if they feel it is too messy. If you have a lot of clutter and you feel this way, then you likely have not had many guests in your house recently. This can cause you to become isolated from the world, especially if you are a homebody. If you like to spend all of your time outside of your home, then I guess this one won't be too relevant for you.

A person who lives in clutter rarely confines these tendencies to their home life. They will carry them everywhere, including their work environment, as you will see with some of the following examples.

You Will Miss Out On Getting Promoted

Untidiness at work, including a messy desk, a chaotic briefcase, or an unorganized filing system, can have negative impacts on your job performance. You will likely spend too much time looking for things and not enough time actually doing any work. Your boss will notice your clutter as well, and this can put you in a bad light when it's time to hand out promotions. According to a study on the career website, CareerBuilder, roughly 28% of employers are less likely to promote someone who keeps their workspace messy. They feel that disorganization leads to poor job performance, and they are right to think this way.

You Are More Likely to Miss Work

The National Institute of Mental Health studies have found that individuals in a cluttered environment are more likely to miss work. They estimated an average of seven missed days per month, which is an excessive number.

Your Productivity Decreases

While you are in a cluttered environment, your ability to focus is severely impeded. If you have many different items within your visual field simultaneously, they all compete for your brain's attention. You cannot give it equally to all of them, so you focus more on things that you are interested in. More often than not, that usually not your work projects. If you have papers, pens, food, and various other things on your desk, you will have a hard time getting any work done at all, and your productivity will be greatly affected. Once again, the bosses will take notice, and you won't be in very high standing when they hand out raises or promotions. In fact, they may not keep you at all if you're not performing as you should.

See how many negative results can happen to your career by keeping your workspace too cluttered? It will behoove you and your career aspirations to change this quickly.

You Will Develop Poor Spending Habits

When you live in a cluttered environment, it can become difficult to find things. As a result, you will buy another item of the same kind, not realizing it was hiding under all of your rubbish.

You Can Go into Debt

This last one may not be relevant anymore due to the ability to make online payments, but those of you who rely on paper bills as a reminder to pay them will suffer greatly. Bills become lost and forgotten, resulting in extra fees. If these are really important bills like credit cards or house payments, then additional problems will occur with the banks and financial institutions. Even your credit score will start to decline.

As you can see, the various negative effects of too much clutter can impact every area of your life. It can significantly decrease your physical and mental health and create many psychological issues for you. With the impact on career and relationships too, you will fall further down into the abyss.

Think about your own life and determine how much of an effect clutter has on your mindset. I am willing to bet that you feel much better sitting in a particular area after you have cleaned it up a little bit. Now that we have established some reasons why people collect clutter and the negative consequences associated with it, I will go over some action steps to get rid of clutter in your life.

Clutter is Not Just Physical

I have spoken a lot about the physical clutter around your home or office. All of this is very distracting and can cause you to lose focus. Too many stimuli will compete for your focus, and you will not be able to give any of them your full attention. Important issues will go right over your head.

Physical clutter is bad, but it is not the only kind you have to contend with. Clutter also includes technology, which is a growing problem in this day and age. We get emails all the time from many different sources. Sometimes we don't even know who the email is from, and just ignore it. However, we often don't erase the email or unsubscribe from the individual, which results in even more unnecessary items in our inbox. Junk email is literally regular junk mail on steroids. When we get so many different ones from various sources, it clutters our files, and we become extremely overwhelmed, just like with physical clutter. As a result, a lot of important information falls through the cracks.

With so much information coming in, it becomes very distracting, and our ability to focus and remain productive decreases. Once we become overwhelmed, we no longer answer emails; we simply scroll through them and hope we did not miss anything important. Suddenly, an important email from our boss comes through, and we never catch it. As a result, critical information was missed, which can jeopardize your company and even your job.

Digital clutter is not exclusive to too many emails. Having an excessive number of programs or apps on your computer, carrying around multiple devices, managing multiple social media accounts, and storing a lot of photos can also be overwhelming in the same manner. In many cases, once a person's data gets used up, they just buy more space, rather than clearing out what they have. It's usually quicker and easier that way. It may not seem like a big deal in the present moment, but after a few months or years, you will realize just how much your productivity and focus has decreased. Increasing productivity and getting things done will be a major topic of this book.

Chapter 2: Breaking Your Relationship With "Stuff"

Now that we have established the psychological reasons people hold onto things, it is to incorporate strategies that will help you get rid of excess clutter. While decluttering can be very difficult at first, it can also be very freeing and have a positive impact on your life in every way. In this chapter, I will go over various different techniques for you to start reducing your personal items or reorganizing them in a proper fashion. Either way, your home, and workspace will become more appealing and habitable.

Getting Over the Endowment Effect

Since the Endowment effect has such a great impact on your ability to get rid of things, I will go over some tips to help you overcome it. Once you go through these steps, you will realize how little value the items in your life actually have and how ridiculous it was to hold onto them for so long when you weren't using them.

The following are a few simple ways to get over the endowment effect:

- Well, now that you know what the endowment effect is, you can become aware that it is personally affecting your life. If you are having difficulty letting go of something you don't need, tell yourself it's the endowment effect and break the curse.

- Using your imagination can help here too. If you are having a hard time getting rid of something, imagine that you do not own it anymore. This can help weaken the emotional ties you have to it.
- Take the items you no longer use and put them in a sealed box. Now, put them somewhere like an attic or basement. Give yourself a timeline, like three months or six months, and if you do not open that box, then give it away without unsealing it.
- Write down your "why." Why is it important for you to declutter, and what value will it bring to your life?

These tips will help you overcome the power that the endowment effect holds on you, and it should become a little easier to declutter your life after this.

More Decluttering Tips

In this section, I will go over some more decluttering tips to help you reorganize your life. You can use one, or all of these, to start getting rid of unnecessary items. Through some of these steps, you can also determine which items you still need and the ones you can get rid of without a thought.

- Make the process less overwhelming if you are new. Start with five minutes a day and use this time to declutter what you can. From here, raise the time at your comfort level.

- Give one item away each day. By the end of week one, you will have given away seven items. By the end of the year, you will have given away 365. You will definitely see your belongings disappearing quickly. If you want to make the process faster, you can certainly increase the amount you give away.
- Get a large trash bag and fill it up with as many items as you can. After filling it up, tie the bag and donate to Goodwill or another donation service before you change your mind.
- Take all of your clothes and hang them facing backward. Whenever you wear an item, hang them back up facing forward. After several months, the clothes that are still facing backward should be donated.
- Use the 12-12-12 rule for getting rid of items. Take out 12 things that you plan on donating, 12 things that you plan to throw away, and 12 things that you will keep for now. This will lessen the impact of getting rid of things because you can see what you're still keeping.
- Go into your home with a first-time visitor mindset. Look around the house and determine how you would clean and reorganize the place, including what items you would get rid of. This is a mind trick you can use to detach yourself from the things inside.
- Choose a small area of your home and take before and after pictures. For example, take a small section on your kitchen counter that has clutter, snap a quick photo, and then clean off the area. Take another photo right after that. Having this visual will help you keep that area clear. Start doing this with other areas of your home too.

Decide whichever tip works best for you and then go from there. If there are others that you come up with, that is fine too. The goal is to declutter in whatever way necessary, so get creative in your approach.

Stop Buying Stuff You Don't Need

If you are decluttering the stuff out of your personal space, but also buying things you don't need at the same time, then it defeats the purpose. You are just replacing one set of items for another. As a result, decluttering will mean nothing as your environment will just become busy again. The goal of decluttering is to keep your space from becoming overfilled. This requires a combination of getting rid of stuff and not buying new stuff. The following are some effective ways to stop buying unnecessary items.

Keep Away from Temptations

If you have a tendency to splurge on things you don't need, then don't tempt yourself by window shopping or going into a store to look around. You might also want to stop getting shopping magazines and cancel online subscriptions to stores. You may not be thinking about buying an item until you see it, and then suddenly, it is in your room just sitting there.

If you must go to the store, make a list and stay laser-focused on it. If you know where the items are, then only go to those sections of the store. You can also shop online and have the items delivered, so you don't actually go out.

Avoid Retail Seduction

Retail stores are masterful at seduction, from hiring the best salespeople, to proper lighting, placement, and layout. All of this is done to draw in their customers, and many people fall for it. This is why someone ends up spending 20 dollars on a coaster set when a five-dollar one would have worked.

Avoid retail seduction by being aware of it. When you see an enticing item, mentally isolate it from its environment and see if the appeal is still there. Also, imagine it being placed in a bin at the thrift store and see if you still want to buy it.

Take Inventory

Oftentimes, we buy things because we don't have enough. However, if you take regular inventory of everything in your home, including inside the drawers, you will find more than you realized. The desire to buy more will go down. Even after you declutter, you will still have many items.

Practice Gratitude

Be mindful of the things you have in your life, both tangible and intangible, and show gratitude for them. Again, you will realize your life is more fulfilling than it appeared beforehand.

These are just a few tips to keep you from going on a shopping splurge and refilling your house with items that are useless. Once you see the powerful effects that decluttering will have on you, it will be lifechanging in so many ways. This is why so many people who became minimalists are much happier now.

Calculate Cost Vs. Labor

The trick here is to figure out how much something costs, and then determine how many hours you would have to work to make up that money. This can really be eye-opening for you. Determine if the labor hours are worth the item you want to purchase.

Keep Your Big Picture in Front of You

When you are spending money day-to-day, it can be easy to lose track of things. You may not realize how much one day of spending can take you away from your ultimate goals. This is why it's important to keep the big picture at the forefront of your mind. Use whatever reminders you need to accomplish this.

A lot of the techniques I have gone over about tricking your mind or shifting the mindset away from what you are used to. Incorporating all of these strategies into your life on a regular basis will give you the best results.

The Benefits Of Decluttering

The benefits of decluttering are another thing you can keep in mind to help you stay focused on eliminating excessive items from your life. The process really is freeing once you give it a chance. The following are a summary of some of the benefits of decluttering. I will get into many more over the next few sections.

- Reduced stress and anxiety related to all of the clutter.
- Reduced number of allergens, like dust, pet hair, and pollen that can accumulate on surfaces.
- A cleaner and more sanitary environment.
- Save extra money and even make money by selling things.
- Extra space in your home for fun activities.
- Less shame in inviting guests.
- Your home will be safer to move around in. There will be fewer things to run into.
- Family or others who are living with you will appreciate it.
- You will realize how many things you can actually do without.

Decluttering Equals Increased Focus and Productivity

Imagine a housecat for a moment. They easily become distracted by shiny lights, new toys, or any hanging objects. If you put something in front of a cat's face, they will be mesmerized by it. If you place multiple items in front of them, they will not be able to figure out which one to focus on. Our minds can become the same way if we let them.

Lucky for us, our brains have a natural filtering mechanism that allows it to not be distracted by every little thing around is. So, when you are performing a task, you may not notice the slight wind outside, the cars driving by on the front seat, or every single person that walks by. Our brains do a great job of shutting out what we don't need to see, hear, or feel every moment.

The problem here is, it takes a lot of energy to filter things out, and this energy is finite. This means that the more things around us that have the potential to catch our attention, the more energy the brain uses, and the more quickly it will dissipate. Therefore, the more clutter you have, the quicker your brain will lose its ability to focus, and you will become distracted more easily.

It is simple to see, then, that decluttering will increase your focus because you have fewer things that will drain the energy required to keep it. Try something as soon as you can. While you are sitting at your table, remove a few items from it and see how many less distractions you have. Remove any objects that are unnecessary to the task at hand. Many people will keep snacks at their desks. Avoid doing this because then you will just be snacking constantly, instead of working. When you're hungry, actually get up, and make yourself something. Put in the work.

Notice how much clearer your mind feels after doing this. When our surroundings become too busy, so does our mind. While some people believe that a busy mind creates productivity, it is quite the opposite. A clear mind with focus is what allows true productivity, so if you want to get things done, clear up your environment, and clear up your brain.

Decluttering and Improved Health

Decluttering will improve many aspects of your health. Notice some of the healthiest people around you, and you will see that their living or workspaces are immaculate compared to others. I will go over a few ways that decluttering will have positive health consequences.

Improved Healthy Habits

When you declutter your home, you will develop healthy habits. The main reason for this is that certain items will be easier to get to and will more likely get used. For example, if you open your closet and quickly find the vacuum or broom, you are more likely to use them. If your vacuum is behind a wall of various items, you will not want to put in the effort to get it. This goes for cooking, as well. If your kitchen is filled up with supplies, like extra appliances, cookware, dirty dishes, and various articles that don't need to be there, you are less likely to cook meals at home. There is a greater chance that you'll just cook a microwave dish or buy fast food.

Better Self-Care

When living in a clean and sanitary environment, you will have better self-care overall. It will be easier and more appealing to exercise in an open space. Also, your sleeping habits will improve because it is easier to be restful in less busy surroundings. Finally, people who declutter slowly develop the habit of remaining clean, which improves hygienic practices.

Losing Weight

This may seem like an odd connection, but it's true. People are much more likely to be overweight if they live in a cluttered environment. A study done by the University of Florida estimates about a 77 percent higher chance of being overweight or obese. This is related to the busy lifestyles that people have, which is common with people who do not declutter. When you learn to declutter, you also learn to slow down. You also become much more organized. This gives you more time to eat properly and exercise.

Easier to Relax

Too much clutter in your home can impact your ability to relax and enjoy yourself. The immense amount of distractions will ever allow your mind to stop getting distracted. It will be hard to immerse yourself in a relaxing activity, like reading, watching a movie, or taking a bath. You will just feel cramped, and trying to calm your nerves will be an uphill batter you cannot win.

All of these benefits will work in conjunction to improve your physical and mental health.

Having More Space

It is easy to see that decluttering opens up space around you. Not only will you have a greater physical area to work in, but a larger mental space to think. You will become more creative because it will be easier for you to open up your mind. This is where some of your best ideas will come into play.

Having an open space can increase your confidence and self-efficacy. A lot of this has to deal with the decluttering process. As you remove items from your life or reorganize them, you will have to make some important decisions. Getting rid of stuff is not easy, and you will have to think quite a bit. This will improve your capability to come up with solutions, which will definitely make you more confident in yourself. This will also give you more energy because you put yourself in the mode of getting things done. This relates back to productivity.

Having more open space reduces family and relationship tension. An excessive mess can lead to major arguments. Disagreements may arise over who causes the clutters, and therefore, who should get rid of it. Parents will often become frustrated with their children because it will take forever to find something. Do not underestimate how beneficial having more open space can be for your personal relationships.

Think back to when you moved into your home or office. This was prior to moving in any furniture or personal items. Even if it's a small space, it certainly looked much bigger than it appeared before adding extra items. Now, imagine how much bigger your space will become from just removing half of your stuff out. You will truly appreciate the extra space when you have it.

6-Week Decluttering Challenge

You can certainly take as long as you need to declutter your home, office, car, or other space that you occupy regularly, but using a challenge can light a fire under and hold you accountable for making some real changes. You can also bring in the help of a friend to help hold you accountable. Let them know what you plan to accomplish each week, and then bring them in at the end of every week to assess your progress. Take before and after photos, too, so you can have your own visuals.

It is a simple process. Starting from the beginning, pick a certain part of your home that you will focus on each week. For example, week one will be dedicated to the kitchen and dining room. Then, the second week will be dedicated to the living room. The third week will be dedicated to one or two bedrooms, depending on the amount of clutter. In the fourth week, the focus will be on the garage. In the fifth week, you can start on the basement. Finally, the sixth week can be used for any leftover closets or the laundry room. This is just an example, and you can make up your own plan based on your particular spaces. You can break down each week into smaller goals, as well.

Here is a visual:

- Week 1: Kitchen and dining room
    - Declutter the countertops-Day 1
    - Declutter the fridge-Day 2
    - Declutter the cabinets-Day 3
    - Declutter the pantry-Day 4
    - Declutter the stove and oven-Day 5
    - Declutter the dining room table-Day6
    - Declutter any other tables or cabinets in the dining room-Day 7

It may be best to start in the kitchen because it is a high traffic area in the house. From here, you can cover the other areas of your home and break it down day by day. It is really that simple. You just have to maintain discipline. Feel free to incorporate any of the strategies for decluttering I went over earlier.

After doing the six-week challenge, give yourself a pat on the back for your accomplishment. You can even reward yourself. In fact, you can also give yourself small rewards at the end of each week, granted that you accomplished what you needed to. If you stick to the challenge, you will not believe how much more space you will have. Your home may even look bigger than before.

Now that we have established the benefits of decluttering and how you can get this done in your life, the rest of the book will cover how to move forward and start getting things done in your life.

PART II

Chapter 1: What is Holding You Back

The first half of this book focused on the negative aspects of clutter and how removing unnecessary items from your life can be cathartic in so many ways. The goal of all of this was to begin getting things done in your life. This includes all aspects of a person's personal and professional life. Honestly, decluttering was just the first step. It was a way to clear up our minds and reduce distractions. After doing this, it is time to start moving forward and getting things done in our lives. Now that our physical and mental spaces are clear, what else can we focus on? The goal of this chapter is to present some of the biggest challenges to getting things done.

Why People Procrastinate

Procrastination is something many people in our society suffer with. It is the purposeful and unnecessary delay of actions or decisions. Why do something now when you can just do it tomorrow? Well, because you never know what tomorrow will bring. Other challenges will arise, distractions will come up, and you will continue to load up your plate because you refuse to take things off of it. Since you are making the excuse today for waiting until tomorrow, what is stopping you from making the same excuse tomorrow, or the next day and the next day?

Imagine being at a buffet and loading up your plate. When you go to sit down, you decide not to eat much of the food because you want it later. Instead, you go and grab another plate to fill up and bring back to the table. Now, you have two plates to finish, and you have no idea how you will do it. Eventually, the restaurant is about to close, and you don't have the time or space to finish everything. You will most likely waste a large portion of the food. This is what procrastination looks like in life. You keep pushing things back until you become overloaded, overwhelmed, and very close to the deadline, if you even make it at all.

Procrastination is one of the worst enemies of getting things done. It really has no value, except for the fact that some people thrive on making quick deadlines. However, you will also be more likely to make big mistakes. You will never be able to complete the work to your full potential because so many things will be missed. Even if they're minor, they still add up.

Procrastination leads to so many missed opportunities too. Several people do not pursue their goals because they put them off for too long. Eventually, they get to the point where they lose interest or become too involved in other things to where they no longer have time.

People assume that procrastination has everything to do with will power. While this can be a major reason, for sure, it is not the only one that exists. There are many deeper reasons for why people put things off. There are some psychological aspects that are at play. For example, anxiety and fear of failure will terrify people into paralysis. Nobody wants to fail, and if they start something, failure is a huge possibility. As a result, we delay starting anything. At least then, we can save face a little bit.

When our motivation to complete a task outweighs the negative aspects, then there's a strong chance we will still finish it. However, if the negative aspects outweigh our own motivation, then we will put off pursuing a goal if we even do so at all. The following are some other factors that keep up from moving forward. If we follow these, we will always procrastinate.

Abstract Goals

If a person has a vague or abstract goal, then they are more likely to procrastinate. They are not excited enough about it. In fact, they might not even know what the goal is, as there is no clear definition. For example, making a promise to get fit is an abstract goal. It is a simple statement with no real substance. What are the chances you will get fit if you have no actual plan in place for doing so? Furthermore, what does "get fit" even mean to? Does it mean losing a certain amount of weight, gaining muscle, looking slimmer, having more energy, or a combination of all? Honestly, you are not even giving yourself a chance to obtain this goal, as you will just put it off until you forget about it.

A more solid goal would be, "I will lose 15 pounds within two months and be able to run six miles by then." This is a concrete goal with real values and end results. From here, you can create specific action steps to get there. For example, losing two pounds and increasing your run mileage by one every week. Once you create real goals with a legitimate plan, then you are more likely to not put things off.

Not Having Foreseeable Rewards

Many individuals put things off because they see no actual rewards in the near future. For example, a teenager may not attend college because he or she cannot fathom waiting four years or more to get a degree in something that might make them money. In addition, the money will not come right away, which is another deterrent.

People often want immediate pleasure rather than long-term success. This can be seen in people neglecting to create savings or investment accounts. They do not want money later; they want it now. As a result, they delay setting up one of these essential accounts because they can't see the benefits they will create in the future.

This same mindset can apply to punishments, as well. The farther into the future a punishment is, the less likely it will motivate someone to take action. If you are studying for a final exam in college and it is months away, you are not that concerned about it, because even if you fail, it will be a while until that actually happens.

A Disconnect from Our Future Selves

People tend to procrastinate because they cannot comprehend a connection between their present and future selves. They believe the two individuals are mutually exclusive for some reason and don't realize that they are creating their future person by the actions you take today.

A person may delay starting a healthy diet because they cannot see themselves overweight and dealing with chronic diseases in the future. A company someone works for has a chance of going out of business, but the employee does not work on his resume because he cannot see himself being out of work. In both of these examples, their present and future selves are completely different people.

Being Too Optimistic

Now, being optimistic is not a bad thing; however, getting to the point where you overthink your abilities can be a problem. This is a common occurrence as many people do not work on tasks in the present because they highly believe they can complete it in the future. While this may be true, there will still be an increased amount of stress and anxiety. Also, the potential for oversight and significant errors will be present.

Imagine that you have a 10,000-word paper due to Friday, and it is only Monday. It would make sense to write 1,000-2,000 words daily, instead of waiting until Wednesday or Thursday. When writing the paper ahead of time, you will have extra opportunities to think everything through, and also go back and edit your work. Giving yourself extra time will help you in creating quality work.

Being Indecisive

This is when you cannot make a move because you cannot decide what course of action to take. For example, you may hesitate to apply for a job because you cannot decide which one is best for you. This is a phenomenon known as analysis paralysis, and it has stopped many great people right in their tracks. The following are some factors that make it difficult to make a decision.

- The more options you have, the harder it will be to decide a preferable path to take.
- The more similar different options are, the harder it will be to choose. You might end up analyzing the smallest sectors of each choice.
- The more important the decision is, the harder it will be to make because of the impact it will have on you and others.

It is best if you can keep your decisions to a minimum, as well as your choices. Each time you make a decision, you deplete your mental resources to a degree. So, if you make a host of decisions in a short time period, you have a high likelihood of getting burned out.

Task Aversion

People often procrastinate because they are not looking forward to a task they need to perform. For example, they might have to call them back to resolve a payment dispute but are not looking forward to talking with a customer service representative. As a result, They put off doing it. If you are avoiding a task because of the aversion you have to it, you are just delaying your agony. Imagine how good you will feel after doing it. So, hold your nose and get it done.

Perfectionism

People often want things so perfect that they are terrified of doing something out of fear of the mistakes they will make. Instead of starting and taking their chances, they avoid moving forward. Perfectionism has been called the enemy of productivity because of all the delays it creates along the way. People do not realize that things will no be perfect, so they waste excessive time trying to ake things this way.

Self-Handicapping

Many individuals are terrified of exposing their lack of ability for something. As a result, they procrastinate so they can use it as an excuse for poor performance. They would rather that people think they're lazy than incapable. Procrastinators with this mindset are more likely to put things off if they feel that failure will reflect badly on them.

These are some of the most common reasons for procrastination. There is no easy answer to why people avoid doing things, but it must be overcome for people to start accomplishing things. The following are a few more reasons for procrastination:

- Self-sabotage
- Low self-efficacy
- Perceived lack of self-control
- Fear of being criticized

Sometimes, there are more urgent situations, like ADHD, depression, or low self-esteem, that need to be addressed. The better question to ask is: Why put something off until tomorrow if I can get it done today?

Other Major Reasons for Not Getting Things Done

For some reason, people are just not getting as many things done as they could. Now, I am not saying you have to be on the go all the time. That is not healthy, either. What I am saying is that you need to accomplish things within a certain time period, or you will never achieve anything in life. This will not just affect you, but those who rely on you, as well, like employees, business partners, and family members. To make the world go around, people need to get things done. Yet, they don't. I already spoke about procrastination as a major factor. I will now detail a few other reasons why this happens.

Not Sure What to do

Many people do not do anything because they have no idea what they should do. Even if they have a goal, they are clueless about how to get started in any way. This often occurs because we see other people's accomplishments but have no idea how they achieved them. We keep trying to guess but can't figure it out. Even if we do become aware of how something was accomplished, the values do not line up with our own, which makes us even more confused. It is better to keep on track with your own beliefs when trying to accomplish a goal, rather than rejecting them completely. Rejecting your values will make you even more confused.

There is No Deadline or Accountability

Accountability seems to be going by the wayside these days. People don't get things done because they are not expected to. There is often no disciplinary actions taken, so people continue to lack the drive to move forwards.

Also, when deadlines are nonexistent, then there is no need to get moving. Either we don't create deadlines for ourselves, or other people don't place them on us. If you work for someone and they do not set deadlines, then the operations of the company are not very sound. If you do not set your own deadlines for goals, then you need to start doing so. Make them concrete and not too far out. Remember, you don't want to fall into a procrastination step.

Set a specific date for when you want to accomplish something and stick to it completely. Set it around important events if you can. For example, if you are planning a vacation or will be attending a concert, make it a goal to finish a certain project or reach a specific endpoint. If you are attending a wedding, and you also need to get in shape to fit into your suit, you can make a goal to lose 10 pounds prior to the wedding.

Don't See Any Consequences

This goes along the lines of accountability, but the reason so many people don't get things done is that they do not realize the consequences until they already occur. For example, if your roof needs to be fixed, you will probably put it off because you do not see any consequences for doing so. Of course, on the night that it's pouring rain and the roof suddenly collapses, you will recognize your mistake. Start seeing the potential consequences of not getting things done. Write them down if you have to. Once you see them visually, then you are more likely to take them seriously. For example, if you need new tires on your car and you have been putting it off, then write down that you will get stranded on the freeway with four ruptured tires.

Why Getting Things Done is Critical

Here is the bottom line. The many advancements we have made in this world were done by go-getters who acted constantly. They were not done by people who refused to do the work. As you look back on history, any type of accomplishment, whether good or bad, had massive action behind it. I say bad, as well, because there have been many negative events in our history. I hope you keep your goals positive.

Getting things done creates a sense of accomplishment. No matter how much or how little you do today, it is far better than doing nothing. Nothing gets you nowhere while small steps create some progress.

Getting things done now is the ultimate productivity hack available. There are no tricks or secret formulas. It is simply a matter of doing something now, rather than nothing at all. Whatever you can manage to do within a given period of time, do it, and you will be that much closer.

Imagine having to paint a house. This is not an easy task, especially if you have a big house. Let's say, for this example, the house has 100 walls to paint. If you pain one a day, that is still something. After 100 days, which is just over three months, you will have painted the whole house. Taking three months is better than nothing at all. On certain days, when you have more time and energy, you can paint extra on those days. If painting your house is a goal, then give yourself a deadline with rewards or punishments along the way. For example, if you are not halfway done by a certain date, then cancel something you were looking forward to. Hold yourself accountable, and if you need to, have someone else hold you accountable too.

In the next chapter, I will cover many different tips to start getting things done.

Chapter 2: It's Time to Get Things Done

Now that I have covered the reason why people don't get things done; it is now time to start taking action. This chapter will be focused on various strategies to overcome the blocks in your life. Start following these, and you will be accomplishing things in no time.

Overcoming Procrastination

It's time to stop putting things off. Many of your dreams and goals have gone unfulfilled because you waited too long to start working on them. The world has also missed out on your gifts because you had the potential to create something great if you only took some action in completing it. The following are some ways to overcome one of the greatest obstacles to not getting something done: Procrastination.

Don't Catastrophize

This means that you make a bigger deal out of things than you should. This could be based on the results you might get, or the excruciating the actual task will be. In any event, you are expecting the process to be unbearable.

Here's a little tip: it won't be. We often overthink to the point that our mind creates a scenario that is not conducive to reality. The truth is, hard work, boredom, and other challenges will not kill you. You may not enjoy them on time, but you will overcome them. Also, the results we get are rarely ever at the level we imagine them to be. The thought of a fall is generally harder than the fall itself.

Always believe in yourself that you can make it through something and deal with the consequences, positive or negative, that come with it. The truth is, you can. Even if a task is as horrible as you imagined, you got through it, and it's out of the way. This is much better than thinking about it. Just get it done!

Focus on Your "Why"

You "why" is the ultimate reason for you doing something and should be used as a motivating factor for you. Many procrastinators focus on short-term gains and do not pay attention to long-term potential. This is why it's important to remember your "why." It is the end result you are expecting.

This can be used for any goal in your life, personal or professional. If you have been putting off creating a resume, then imagine yourself in your dream job. If you have been putting off organizing your room, imagine how good you will feel when you can find things easily and don't have to get around a huge mess.

Get Out Your Scheduler

Projects often do not get done because people make no time for them. They will do it when they have time, and therefore, the time will never come. You need to make time and stick to it. Get out your scheduler, whether it's an online planner, paper planner, or calendar, and start blocking off times. Whatever important tasks that need to be completed, write them down and on a specific time and date. Unless something unavoidable comes up, stick to the specific block on your schedule. When people write things down, they are holding themselves accountable. If they miss doing something, they can look at it, and it will remind them.

Be Realistic

Getting things done means you are setting yourself up for success. Do not create unrealistic goals for yourself. Set an achievable goal, and then take specific action steps to get there. For example, do not tell yourself that you will start working out five times a week in the morning immediately when you are not even a morning person. Instead, set up your workout schedule in the evening. If you ultimately want to work out in the mornings, then you can start by doing it once a week and then increasing your days. Do not expect to reach your goals instantly. Set up a long-term plan for success.

Break it Down

Tasks can often become overwhelming, and this leads to procrastination. Break them down into smaller and more manageable tasks with specific deadlines for each small task. If you are planning to landscape your home, start with a small area and give yourself the time you need in each section.

Stop With the Excuses

Here it goes: You will never be fully energized; it will never be the right time; you will often not be in the mood; conditions may never be perfect. Stop using these as excuses. Waiting for any of these will just delay you for no reason. Getting things done is not about waiting for the perfect opportunity. It is about using what you ave to create opportunity. Stop with the excuses!

Find an Accountability Partner

It can be difficult to hold yourself accountable, so find a partner to help you. Express what your goals are to this person and the deadlines that you have. Your accountability partner can then follow up with you and make sure you are staying on track. If you don't reach your deadlines, your partner's job is to grill you as to why. You guys can help each other in this manner to make it a mutual relationship.

Optimize Your Environment

Your environment will play a huge role in creating distractions. Optimize it by finding a quiet place and only having the things you absolutely need. Turn off the TV, social media (I recommend logging out so you can't access it easily), get rid of any papers or clutter that will catch your attention. How many times have you meant to start something, only to get distracted by something else? This is very common, and you must do what you can to avoid it happening to you.

Forgive Yourself

While it might be true that starting something earlier would have been more advantageous, do not beat yourself up for not doing so. You cannot change the past, so forget about it. You can make up for it though by taking advantage of the present. Learn from your past mistake of putting something off and start doing things today. If you should have gone to college five years ago, well, it's okay. You can still go now.

Procrastinators are often trying to avoid distress, but in doing so, they are ironically creating more of it. Start taking the action steps I have described above, and you will no longer be putting things off until tomorrow.

Mindfulness Meditation Technique

Many individuals are not able to get things done because they cannot live in the present moment. They are either anxious about the past or worried about the future. Both of these are unproductive thoughts to have and must be eliminated immediately. You must start focusing on the present, and mindfulness meditation techniques are a great way to do so. Bear in mind, it can take years to master the practice of meditation, so I will just go over the basics to get you started. The following are some structured meditation exercises.

Body Scan Meditation

Start by lying down on your back with your arms at your sides, palms facing up, and legs extended. Now pay close attention and observe every section of your body from head to toe. Become fully aware of any sensations or emotions you are feeling and from where they are coming from. This will bring awareness to yourself and what is happening to you. You will begin living in the present moment with real-time feelings.

Sitting Meditation

Sit in a comfortable position, preferable in a chair, with your back straight, feet flat on the floor, and your palms on your lap. Once in a comfortable position, breathe in slowly through your nose and allow it to go down to your diaphragm. Then slowly let the breath out. Focus completely on your breathing. If you get distracted by anything, note the experience and then return your attention back to your breathing.

Walking Meditation

Find a quiet space that is at least 15-20 feet in length. Walk slowly between each wall in the room and focus completely on the experience. Be aware of all of the subtle movements that are being used to keep you balanced. Do not pay attention to anything else but your walking.

Simple Mindfulness

The following are a few more mindfulness exercises. These are simple and can be practiced anywhere.

- Focus on your breathing. Take slow and deep breaths in and out. This was done in the meditative position but can also be accomplished standing up anywhere.
- Find joy in the simple pleasures of life and live in the moment.
- Accept yourself and learn to treat yourself like you would a good friend.
- Experience the environment you are in with all of your senses. Do not be in such a rush all the time. Fully taste the food you're eating, stop to smell the roses, listen to the birds chirping, and even touch some dirt. Feel your surroundings.

15 Habits of Highly Productive People

To become successful, you must mimic the habits of other successful people. The following are effective habits that productive people use every day. These individuals get things done, and you can, as well.

- Focus on the most important tasks first. These are the ones that have the most urgency, the closest deadlines, and the most with the most severe results if not done. Complete them first and then move on to other things.

- Cultivate deep work, which are your hardest, most boring, and most complicated tasks. They have to be done, and if you are not focused fully, they will be missed. Say "no" to people more often, limit distractions, set up a scheduled time for these tasks each day, and go where you do your best work, whether in the office, library, or café, etc.

- Keep a distraction list. While you are working, anytime a distraction comes up, write it down, and then get back to work. This technique works because you are giving attention to your distraction, which eases up its strength over you.

- Use the 80/20 rule. Determine the 20% of your work that requires the most attention. Look at the remaining 80% and see what you can cut out to make more time for the 20%.

- Take scheduled breaks. Even though you want to get a lot done, you cannot just work 24/7. Take scheduled breaks throughout your workday and spend the rest of the time being fully focused. For instance, spend 55 minutes working hard, then take a 10 minutes break to relax and eat something.

- Limit the number of decisions you have to make. Decisions that aren't important should not take up too much of your time or energy. For example, many productive people will wear similar outfits every day because their wardrobe is not as important as other decisions.

- Eliminate insufficient communication. Ignore and delete useless emails, do not engage in too much idle chatter, and avoid gossip, which is a complete waste of time.
- Delegate certain tasks when you can. If you are busy with your career, then you can hire people to do things like take care of your lawn or do your dry cleaning.
- Learn from your successes, as well as your mistakes. Even in success, lessons can be learned about making things more efficient.
- Plan as much as you can for things going wrong because getting caught off guard can be quite a time consumer. It is better to have a plan ahead of time than trying to come up with one urgently.
- Don't wait until you are inspired or motivated to work. Start working and get yourself inspired or motivated.
- Avoid Multitasking. Instead, focus on one task for as long as you can before moving over to the next one.
- Get enough sleep, eat well, exercise, and take time to recharge. This will give you the energy you need when it's time to be productive. Whenever you do something, put all of your effort into it, including rest.
- Take time to get better at tasks by educating yourself and improving your skills.
- Manage your time and energy. Do not waste any of them unnecessarily.

Once you start taking these action steps seriously, you will notice yourself accomplishing a lot more. I will now get into looking towards your future and the life you want to create.

Chapter 3: Visualizing a Better Future

When you learn to get things done and do them well, you will create a better future for yourself. This can become one of your motivations to get moving, as well. In this chapter, I will continue to focus on action steps to get you moving so you can get things done. Once you can visualize your future, you can create it.

How to Visualize Your Future

In this section, I will go over some ways to visualize your future so that you can create an image that inspires you. This is a powerful tool that helps you create the future you want. Will it turn out exactly as you see it? Definitely not. There are too many variables that factor in. However, always keeping that picture in mind means that you will push yourself harder to achieve the success you want. As you see your reality a few years down the line, you will expect more out of yourself. Start by answering the following questions. Remember, these are the answers you hope to give five, 10, 15, or whatever years down the line.

- When someone asks you what you do for work, what do you tell them?
- Describe all of your surroundings in great detail, including your house, the city, neighborhood, and what's nearby. Where do you spend most of your free time?
- What is the atmosphere like at work and in your home, and how do you contribute to it?
- What is your greatest accomplishment? What brings you the most pride?

- Are there any regrets that you have?
- What are the specific steps you took to get where you are?
- What advice would you give to someone else who wants to be where you are?
- What problems arose along the way?

After answering these questions, you will understand where you want to be and have an idea of how to get there.

More Tips for Visualization

Once you begin visualizing your future, then you have it ingrained in your mind. It becomes much harder to let it go. Of course, this does not mean that it's a guarantee. You still must put in the work and make the right moves. For example, if you want to start a business, you can picture the type, how big it will be, where it should be located, how it will look, and whether you plan to have employees or not, among other things. Seeing is believing, though, and the following tips will help you start believing in yourself and your future.

Visualize Your New Life

One way to become excited about your goals is to imagine what your life will be like when you achieve them. For example, if you plan on increasing your salary, imagine that extra money coming in. How much will it be, and what will you be able to do with it? What will you be doing to get that extra money, whether it's through work, investing, or starting a business, etc.? Anything you can imagine about what your life will be like, try to picture it in your mind.

Create a Vision Board

Start collecting images, quotes, articles, and any other visual representations that you feel reflect your future. For instance, you can collect a specific item from a state if you plan on living there someday. This will help you trigger inspiration and hold you accountable for your dreams.

Write Down Your goals

This is a common practice and is touted as being very effective by most productive people. If you are not fond of vision boards, you can write down your goals in lieu of that practice. You may also do it in conjunction with each other for added benefits.

Let Yourself Zone Out

If you find yourself daydreaming at certain times, let it happen. Your mind is trying to tell you something about what you want. Many geniuses in the past, including Einstein, would zone out throughout the day. During these moments, a bolt of inspiration can strike, and great plans can be made. Of course, you cannot daydream all the time, or nothing will get done, which defeats the purpose.

However, when you can, take the time to do it.

Say Your Goals Out Loud

Whatever you have planned, whether short-term or long-term, say it out loud, so the universe knows. This also triggers your brain to understand what you want, so it also starts thinking towards that direction.

Think About What You Want and not What You Don't Want

There is a phenomenon known as the Law of Attraction. According to the rules, what you focus on is what the universe delivers to you, even if you're thinking about it in a negative way. So, even if you're thinking about poverty in terms of not falling into it, you will still attract it because it is in your mind. Therefore, it is better not to even visualize poverty but just think about becoming wealthy.

Life When You Get Things Done

All the information and strategies I have gone over in this book lead up to one thing: Getting things done. That is how you achieve what you want in life. You simply must take action and go for what you want. The action steps in the previous chapters provide a way to make goal-getting easier by providing direction, focus, and motivation. I will end this book by over the many benefits of getting things. Getting things done, or GTD is an actual process and state of mind. When you start incorporating it, you will notice many changes during and after.

A Feeling of Relaxed Control

You will feel in control of your life because you are taking active steps to create it. This may be the number one benefit of getting things done. Performing frequent assessments, processing information, and acting on it can make your mind feel like it's water, where it just flows and makes decisions naturally. It takes time for everyone to get to this state.

Your Thinking Will Be Stimulated

When you get things done, your thinking will be stimulated in advance. You will continuously be thinking about the little and big projects in your life, and they will rarely if ever, slip by you. Procrastination will be an afterthought, and you will always be ahead of the curve.

More Organization and Less Clutter

Getting things done means you will clean off your desk literally and figuratively. You will accomplish your tasks and keep your work area organized too. When you get things done, you will be more versatile, and it will become easier to make and keep commitments. In addition, you will be able to keep others accountable for their commitments.

Less Time for Worry

Thinking is good, but overthinking can be detrimental. It can lead to worry, anxiety, and fear. One of the best ways to avoid this is by acting. Worrying occurs when you have a moment for it. When you act, you are doing and have less time to worry.

The entire point of getting things done is just that, getting things done. This is how you accomplish your goals and start living the life you imagine. There are so many get-rich-quick schemes and people promising others the world if they just do a few simple things. With this book, I wanted to provide many different action steps for you so you can tidy up, clear out unnecessary garbage, both emotional and physical, and start working on your dreams. It may take time, but if you're moving in the right direction, that is what matters most.

PART III

Chapter 1: Back to the Basics

When most people think of mindfulness, they envision monks or yogis, sitting cross legged for hours with closed eyes and poised fingers overlooking the Himalayas. Although mindfulness is present in the lives of monks and yogis, what most people don't know is how easy it is to incorporate mindfulness into our everyday lives. As a matter of fact, a mindful state is the most natural and restful state for human beings—a state in which we were all living and moving in as children. If you think back to your childhood, you will likely remember that your concept of time and perception of reality was much different. Most children are very in touch with their emotions, letting them come and go naturally. If a child falls down in one moment and skins their knee, the child will likely begin to cry. However, if a few moments later they are being offered ice cream, their tears will dry, and they will continue on with their day. Mindfulness is the reason children are so in tune with the details of life that adults seem to miss. It is also the reason they are more likely to screech with joy, run around excitedly in enjoyable environments, wake up easily in the morning, and take the time they need to calm down from anger or sadness until the next happy moment arises. Children spend very little time thinking about things beyond the present moment. Even if they have something to look forward to, they are still likely to become invested in the moment at hand, whether that is playing, enjoying time with their parents, or eating a meal. So, what happens as people grow older that brings us away from this natural state of mindfulness?

There are a number of factors that pull people out of the present moment. From the time a child begins elementary school, they are presented with a schedule for the day, which remains relatively the same. Children are expected to remain within the structures presented to them, and the idea of forward-thinking and preparing for the next hour's activity becomes introduced. As they grow, children will likely have more expectations placed upon them, whether those expectations are academic, extracurricular, or within the home. Of course, it is necessary for children to learn how to be responsible and dedicate the time they need to the important things in life. However, as they become further exposed to the constant rush and future-oriented thinking of their parents and teachers, they come to see time as something that no longer belongs to them to fully inhabit.

Furthermore, as people approach teenage and young adulthood, they will begin to face challenges that most children are either shielded from or otherwise unaware of. People become flooded with the pressure to perform well and always be doing more today than yesterday. Although the expectations of cultures and societies vary, we can be sure that people are overwhelmed with the pressure to meet those expectations in order to be considered successful and valid. Once one bar is crossed, another one is waiting, and there is no time to slack. Additionally, the older people become, the more likely they are to be subject to long-lasting pain in their lives. This can come in the form of relationships ending, failing to accomplish something, being mistreated by other people, losing and grieving loved ones, or coming to terms with painful childhood events that did not make sense at the time. Teenagers become increasingly subject to mental health issues as they advance into adulthood, having to face all of the hard realities of the world and still come out on top. People may also be subject to trauma as a result of illness, accident, or abuse. All of these factors are enough to work against people and pull them out of the present moment, either because it is too painful to be there, or because they are simply too distracted.

Human beings experience over 60,000 thoughts per day, but the vast majority are dedicated either to planning for the future or worrying about the past. Becoming overly concerned about the future or steeping in the pains or regrets of the past can increase levels of stress in the body, which makes people more anxious and prone to physical health problems.

The mind naturally wanders, and it is impossible to keep thoughts from coming. Mindfulness is not a tool to eradicate such thoughts, as is the common misconception. Rather, it is a tool through which to acknowledge the thoughts the mind creates, bring attention to them, and allow them to move through. This ultimately brings people into what is happening here and now and gives them more control over their minds and how they orient themselves in their environments.

Because mindfulness is a skill that all human beings are equipped with at our core, it is something that can be re-learned. Just as we exercise our bodies to strengthen our muscles, so we must work to strengthen our brain through mindfulness. The way this strengthening happens is through being aware of thoughts as they arise, then breathing back into the present moment. The more practice is given to returning to the present moment, the stronger the mind will become in remaining in the present more often. Just as the body physically strengthens and becomes healthier over time with exercise, mindfulness exercises can physically change the structure of the brain to make it healthier. Mindfulness activates the positive components of the hippocampus, which is the part of the brain responsible for good things like creativity, joy, and the ability to process emotions. This, in turn, decreases stress levels, depressive tendencies, addictive behaviors, and the fight or flight instinct by shrinking the part of the brain responsible for negative things (the amygdala). Overall, increased mindfulness is the key to a longer, healthier, more creative, and more joyful life.

Chapter 2: Unlocking Your True Purpose Through Mindfulness

Re-centering Yourself

Everyone has days where everything seems to be spinning out of control, and there seems to be no way to manage the chaos. The days where you wake up late, run late to work, spill coffee on your shirt, get cut off on the road, get yelled at by your boss, spend the entire day at work in a confused frenzy, only to come home and bicker with your partner. Since the beginning of time, the human mind has been conditioned to release stress hormones and illicit the fight or flight instinct for the purpose of protection and survival. In the past, this primal instinct was very useful for escaping threats. As times have changed, the threats have become less severe, but the brain's response has remained largely the same. Now, these fight or flight reactions are likely to be triggered by everyday scenarios, such as those previously detailed. The hormone-induced responses that occur when we're stressed out are quick to send us spiraling into emotionally dramatic, and far less peaceful dimensions.

The good news is, mindfulness can be used as a tool for re-centering and gaining control over your anxiety and emotional reactions when you start to feel yourself spiral. Although there is no way to avoid stress and drama in daily life, mindfulness can serve as a shield of calm presence to protect your well-being. If you are preparing to enter a situation that you anticipate could be stressful, like a high-stakes day at work, a scary doctor's appointment, or a difficult conversation with a loved one, it can be incredibly helpful to bring yourself down to a more calm and balanced state in preparation for the stress you are about to deal with. You may find yourself with a racing heart, sweating palms, an unclear head, and the feeling of "butterflies in your stomach." Another area where it is common to feel these physical effects of anxiety is when encountering dramatic situations. Drama can arise tense moments with other people, as well as within the theoretical situations people create for themselves when worrying about what they cannot control (for example, the perception other people have of them, or events that may or may not occur in the future). Giving attention to what is happening in your mind and body and allowing yourself to breathe into the moment can be a total lifesaver in moments of drama or stress. Two to three minutes of deep breathing in your car before going to work, or taking a few deep breaths before reacting in a tense moment, can make a drastic difference in your sense of balance and your ability to deal with stress without launching into fight or flight.

Giving Your Emotions Space

The goal of mindfulness is not to eliminate emotions, but rather, to gain control over the impact they have on how we orient ourselves in the world. It is vital to honor our emotions and give them space to exist and teach us, without letting them seize control. Mindfulness is an excellent tool for giving our emotions space in this way. When an emotion arises, mindfulness gives us a chance to observe that emotion without judgment. In this calm space, we can ask our emotions, "What are you trying to teach me?" We can more clearly discern why we are experiencing a certain emotion, and become in touch with the deeper needs that may have caused that emotion to arise. Just as a child may cry when they need to be nourished our held, we may find ourselves growing angry or agitated when we need support, touch, or self-care. Similarly, we may find ourselves feeling stressed or anxious in scenarios that are subconsciously triggering moments from the past. In these cases, our stress and anxiety are begging us to become in touch with our past self, reminding ourselves that we are safe, and the traumatic moments from the past are over. Once our emotions have been given a non-judgmental space to exist, they can smoothly and peacefully move through the body and be released. This frees us to move from moment to moment like children do, without being constrained by unresolved emotions. Additionally, giving this space to our emotions in mindfulness helps to temper our reactions, which can prevent us from acting out in extreme ways and potentially doing or saying something we regret.

Making Clear Decisions

With the human mind constantly being muddled with thoughts, it can be hard to see things clearly. Sometimes our minds are cluttered by the expectations flying at us from every different direction, or perhaps by our fears of what will happen if things don't go to plan. When it comes to making decisions, we are often faced with numerous options, and it can be difficult to navigate through the chaos in our minds to come to a well thought out resolution. In a distracted, anxious, or removed state, our minds are like a pond on a rainy day—rippling to a point where there is no more clarity. Mindfulness is the calming of the waters, which brings us to a place where we can more clearly think of all possible outcomes of a decision and check in with what we truly need before moving into the next moment.

Keeping Yourself Safe

Although fight or flight instincts originally developed as a way to keep humans safe, in many modern-day scenarios, they do quite the opposite. Let's go back to the example from the beginning of the chapter about the chain of events in a typical chaotic day. If you wake up late in the morning and rush to make your coffee, not paying attention to what you are doing, you run the risk of haphazardly screwing the lid on your to-go cup, then sloshing boiling hot coffee over the edge of the cup and onto yourself as you bolt out the door. Although such a scenario could simply result in a stained shirt, the inattentiveness could have a more drastic effect, such as burning yourself or someone else. Driving to work in a state of panic over running late causes you to be more likely to break the rules of the road—driving too fast, making dangerous decisions when changing lanes, taking turns too fast, running yellow lights just before they turn red, etc. Additionally, the panicked state can lead to anger with yourself or others on the road, which can further impair judgment and put you at greater risk of an accident. Attempting to have a conversation with your boss if you are in fight or flight mode could result in being overly emotional and saying or doing something extreme which could place you at odds within your workplace, potentially even costing your position. Going throughout your day in a frenzy causes you to be less aware of what is going on around you, which can lead to further threats to safety like leaving a burner on, forgetting to eat or drink enough water, or neglecting those in your care (such as pets or children) as a result of your own inner distractions. Finally, as stress from the day carries into the home at the end of the day, it can pose a major threat to relationships. The more stressed out and less clear thinking you are, the more likely you are to say or do something threatening to your partner, to put yourself in an aggressive and volatile situation, and to make brash decisions that have the potential to haunt your future.

Improving Relationships

Just as we must give ourselves space to learn, grow, and process our experiences, we must give that space to those around us as well. When a partner or friend is acting in a way we don't enjoy, mindfulness can allow us to take a step back and look at the situation from a position of empathy. We can allow ourselves to hold space for whatever that person may be going through individually and express our support while also maintaining boundaries and staying in control of what we can. Everyone is deserving of space to be listened to, understood, and supported for who they are. However, it is incredibly difficult to give that space to anyone if it has not been cleared within oneself.

When we operate out of a mindless state, there is hardly any space to meet our own needs and process our own experience, much less to provide that to other people. This can lead us to be closed off to the ones we love, push them away, or act out in anger, selfishness, or aggression. If we have not given space to what is going on within us, we cannot offer full empathy to others. Only 20% of the population is recorded to practice true empathy, which can be linked to the rarity of true mindfulness among adults. Mindfulness allows us to be more present to our own needs in order to hold adequate space for the needs of others as well.

Attention and mutual respect are core elements of every functional relationship. Practicing mindfulness can improve relationships with all the people in our lives by preparing us for every engagement and calming our minds enough to be fully present in the moments we share with others. Mindfulness clears the space for us to listen intentionally to other people and pay more attention to what kind of people they are and what kind of support they need. It allows us to love other people better by increasing our awareness of how they feel most loved. By being present in the moment at hand, as opposed to trapped in the past or future, you are more likely to remember to pick up the phone and give your grandmother a call, to be fully engaged when interacting with your child, or to remember the kind of kombucha your significant other likes best from the store. Not only does mindfulness allow for more meaningful conversations and joyful memories, but it also increases the functionality of our relationships overall so that both ourselves and those we love are feeling fully respected, listened to, and encouraged.

Fostering True Joy

We often hear the term "childlike joy" to describe moments of pure bliss, enthusiasm, and full satisfaction. As people grow into adults, such moments tend to be few and far between, with many remembering the most joyful moments to have been those that occurred in childhood. The expectations of daily life become too much, and most people find themselves trapped in a cycle of constant anticipation. People spend so much time thinking about where they would rather be (on vacation, in bed, enjoying the weekend) that the days melt into each other without us realizing all the moments of our lives we are missing. The biggest societal misconception is that true happiness lies in what we do not yet have. We are flooded with lies such as "Once I can buy this new TV, then I'll be happy," or, "Once I have a partner, then I'll be happy," or, "I'll be happy once I can say I've been to five different countries." Mindfulness abolishes these lies by proving to us that the capacity for true joy lies not in the future but in the here and now. Wherever you are right now, whatever you have, and whichever stage of life you're in, mindfulness reminds you that *this* is your chance to experience beauty and satisfaction like never before. Take time to look at the flowers you did not notice growing in front of your neighbor's house, the complexity of coffee's flavor as it slides down your throat, the way your loved one's eyes crinkle when they smile, the laughter of a child, every intricate flavor of dinner, or the unique people wandering up and down the streets you drive every day to work. It is here that joy resides; all you have to do is be present enough to recognize it.

Chapter 3: Moving Mindfully in Daily Life

Coming to the Present Moment: Daily Guided Mindfulness Meditation With Journaling (Week 1)

Cultivating Mindfulness

This meditation should be done in a space where you feel fully comfortable, safe, and relaxed. Perhaps it is in a corner of your bedroom, in a garden, by your favorite lake, or even in your car. Make sure you can fully relax and avoid distractions. Some people meditate best with instrumental music or nature sounds in the background, while others prefer silence. Feel free to try multiple methods and see which is most soothing to you (this can vary depending on the day). You may do this meditation sitting in a chair, on a mat, or lying flat on your back with your palms up to the sky. You will need to give yourself 5-20 minutes of time to practice, depending on your skill level and current state. If you like, you can set a timer.

Start by coming into the moment with a few deep breaths. Settle into your body and take note of any sensations you feel. If you feel pain, tingling, warmth, or tightness in any part of your body, focus your breath into that space. Imagine any tension unfurling into openness. Notice as your thoughts arise. Take notice of them, then allow them to pass as you come back to the breath. If it is helpful, you can try a breathing pattern in order to culminate focus. To do the 4-4-4 breathing pattern, breathe in for 4 counts, hold for 4 counts, and breathe out for 4 counts. To do the 5-5-7 breathing pattern, breath in for 5 counts, hold for 5 counts, release for 7 counts. Sometimes it helps to imagine breathing in the things you wish to see more of in your daily life (creativity, love, patience, openness) and exhale the negative things (fear, negativity, sadness, stress). Allow yourself to spend a few moments in a more active state of breathing in, releasing, and paying attention to your body.

With practice, you may enter a state where your thoughts slow and you become fully grounded in the present moment. In this state, you are no longer bombarded with thoughts, nor distracted by elements of your environment. It becomes easier to return to the breath. All restlessness and tension in the body seem to melt away, and the mind reaches a flowing, liquified state. There may be days when you cannot enter into this state, and you remain restless throughout the course of the meditation. If this happens, allow it to be that way, observing every thought that arises, then letting it go.

After the time is up, begin to arrive in the moment by moving your body slightly—wiggling your fingers and toes, tensing and releasing your muscles, etc. Next, you're your eyes. Notice how bright and clear the world looks to mindful eyes. Notice the calm, transcendent feeling in your body, and continue to move with it as you go about your day.

Mindfulness Meditation Journal Prompt (Week 1):

What did you feel in your body before beginning? What do you feel now?

Which thoughts continued to arise in your consciousness? Could these thoughts have been trying to teach you something or speak to a deeper need you may have?

How does the world look after opening your eyes? What do you notice?

Come back after going about your day for several hours. Did you bring mindfulness with you into the world? If so, how?

Coming to the Present Moment: Daily Guided Mindfulness Meditation With Journaling (Week 2)

Taking Mindfulness Into the World

This meditation will be done with your eyes open in moments if your daily life. This is not a specific meditation you have to set aside time for, but rather a state you come into. Notice where your attention goes in a given moment. If your attention is drawn to a particular sight, like the nearest tree or a view from the top of a mountain, allow yourself to see it fully. Repeatedly tell yourself, "see, see, see." Breathe as you allow your eyes to truly become totally focused and take in the image fully, allowing it to become a part of your awareness.

If your attention is drawn to an auditory experience, such as the sound of cars on a city street, a rushing body of water, or an internal monologue, give full attention to that thing. Soak in that auditory experience, breathing slowly and telling yourself, "hear, hear, hear."

You may also be drawn to a particular physical or emotional experience within the body. This experience may be positive, like a pleasant bodily sensation or a feeling of joy. It may also be negative, like physical pain, or feelings of anger or feel. Either way, allow yourself to become fully present with what is there, breathing into the experience and seeing what it has to teach you. Breathe into that bodily experience, telling yourself, "feel, feel, feel."

Throughout the day, you'll find that your attention is pulled in various directions. Mindfulness is the choice to tune in to whichever place you're going in a given moment and give full attention to that experience for whatever it is.

Mindfulness Meditation Journal Prompt (Week 2):

How difficult was it to bring mindfulness into your daily life in this way? Where did you face the most challenges?

Did your attention tend towards certain experiences (visual, auditory, bodily) more than others?

Describe a specific moment where you brought mindfulness to your experience and felt truly present. What did you observe?

Coming to the Present Moment: Daily Guided Mindfulness Meditation With Journaling (Week 3)

Mindfulness at Work (or School)

The first part of this meditation should happen in a place outside of work, where you feel safe, calm, and separated from the issues you may face in the workplace. Start by identifying your biggest struggles at work. The journal portion will give you a space to write them down. Do you struggle with productivity? Boredom? Stress? Conflict resolution? Work relationships? Once you have identified your most significant area(s) of struggle, close your eyes and visualize what that unpleasant experience looks like. Perhaps it looks like you, rushing around mindlessly like a bee in a hive, stressed out and too overbooked to step away and breathe because there are more calls to make, more e-mails to send, more things to do. Or, perhaps it is the co-worker, professor, or boss that makes your stomach drop whenever you think about having to interact with them. Perhaps you feel unfulfilled at work and find yourself constantly checking the clock, thinking about the moment you get to leave. Maybe you have so many things to do and no idea where to start, so you waste a lot of time on mindless tasks. Whatever your struggles at work are, use your time and space away from work to safely visualize the situation. Breathe into the mental circumstance.

As you breathe, begin to envision what this experience would look like if it went the way you want it to. Perhaps it looks like the mental clarity that allows you to know exactly what needs to get done and how to make the best possible use of your time. It could be a greater sense of calm and courage when talking with your difficult boss or co-worker and having your message be well-received on their end. It may also be a deeper sense of satisfaction and enjoyment in the work you're doing, providing you the ability to step back and feel a sense of joy with where you're at, without constantly thinking about the next thing. Reframe the moment in your mind until you've created a mental space that feels good. Let yourself sit there, breathing, soaking it in for several minutes.

Once you go into the workplace (or school), you can bring this meditation into your life by going back to the peaceful mental image you've created over and over again. When you begin to feel stressed, bored, anxious, or unproductive, return to the space where you do not feel those things. Bring that energy into your daily work life, and watch how it revolutionizes your experience.

Mindfulness Meditation Journal Prompt (Week 3):

What do you identify as your biggest challenge(s) at work or school?

How does it look when you reframe your struggles to create a positive mental image?

What do you observe about bringing this positive mental image into difficult situations in the workplace or at school?

Mini Meditation Toolbox: 15 Quick and Easy Meditations to Integrate Mindfulness Into Your Daily Life

One-Minute Mindfulness

- Find a space where you can be alone, like on your bathroom break or in your car right before going into work, school, or home at the end of the day.
- Set a timer for one minute
- Close your eyes and focus exclusively on your breathing
- Take notice of the stresses, thoughts, and anxieties that arise, then let them go
- When you open your eyes, notice how you feel de-stressed, clear-minded, and prepared to go about your upcoming tasks and interactions with others

5-Minute Body Scan

- Set a timer for 5 minutes (if needed)
- Close your eyes and take several deep, cleansing breaths. You may use the 4-4-4 or 5-5-7 breathing patterns to deepen the breath
- Begin to bring attention to your body
- Take notice of any sensations that arise-- warmth, tingling, tension, etc.
- Bring your attention to the soles of the feet. Tighten your muscles by curling your toes, then release. What sensations do you feel?

- Continue moving up the body to your calves, hips, abdomen, chest, hands, arms, face, and neck. Observe any sensations that arise, and breathe into those sensations.
- Tighten and release the muscles in each of these areas, allowing any pent-up energy or resistance to be released
- Feel your body become grounded, relaxing completely into the floor, bed, or chair as you come into the present moment in your body and all tension melts away

Mindful Bath/Shower (10-minute meditation)

- As you begin your bath or shower, take a moment to breathe. Remove yourself from the stresses of the day and allow yourself to re-center
- Bring attention to each part of your body as you wash it
- Take notice of any sensations you feel as you move from the soles of your feet to the ends of your hair
- Breathe in the pleasant scent of the soaps and the warmth of the water. Allow yourself to feel clean, warm, and safe.
- As you wash each part of your body, thank it for what it does for you. Then, thank yourself for taking care of your body.

Mindful Morning Routine (15-30 minutes)

- Before getting out of bed, begin to stretch gently, letting thoughts come and go as your mind and body wake up. Do not rush yourself.
- Once you are ready to get out of bed, bring your attention to the space around you and the day ahead. Feel yourself become fully present in that space and prepared to move mindfully through your day
- Pay attention to every move you make, from putting on clothes, to washing your face, to setting the water on the stove to boil.
- Cultivate your awareness for the day ahead by moving slowly and calmly, one task at a time, becoming fully awake to the world

Mindful Housekeeping

- Allow yourself to become focused on the task at hand and only that task. Let every other thing you have to do or think about fade into the background.
- Bring your attention to the breath and the specific way your body moves as you complete a particular task or chore
- Give space to any thoughts or emotions that arise in your consciousness, allowing yourself to process them in a mindful state

Mindful Sit-and-Drink (10-minute meditation)

- Find a calm, quiet space where you can sit and observe the world around you (preferably outside or near a window looking outside)
- Pour a glass of your favorite tea, coffee, or cocktail to enjoy
- Eliminate all distractions. Draw your attention to the intricate flavors of the drink, and the pleasure of pulling something you enjoy into your body
- Take notice of the things happening around you. Find the things in the environment that bring you the most peace, and allow their presence with you to help you calm your mind. Become completely indulged in the moment.

Mindful Scheduling (10-minute meditation)
- Sit down with a pen and paper and center yourself with five deep breaths.
- Think about the days to come. Consider your priorities, remembering that every task is significant and an opportunity for increased mindfulness
- Ask yourself, "Am I giving myself adequate time to bring mindfulness and intentionality into each of these activities?"
- Take notice of any activities you feel you won't be able to be fully present for. Consider taking a thing or two off the list and saving them for a better time.
- Take notice of any feelings of stress, nervousness, or rush you feel in regards to your schedule. Breathe into those feelings.

- As you continue to write your schedule, allow yourself to feel empowered, in control, and prepared to be mindful of everything you are about to do

Mindful Driving

- Leave the house with plenty of time to be relaxed and focused. After entering the car, take a few moments to breathe and center yourself
- Once you start to drive, begin to take note of the things passing by. What do you see today that you did not see yesterday?
- Breathe in your visual surroundings, using them to center and remind yourself: "I am here. I am in this community. This is my life, and I am awake to it."

Mindful Walking (10-20-minute meditation)

- Choose an area where you can relax and bring attention to your surroundings. This can be in a park, in the city, on the beach, in your neighborhood, etc.
- Set out on your walk with no distractions
- Take notice of the things your eyes fall upon. If something specific catches your attention, allow yourself to pause and breathe it in.
- Pay attention to the sounds that surround you, giving yourself space to truly hear them

- Pay attention to the feeling of your feet on the pavement, the swing of your arms at your sides, and the rhythm of your breath
- Let your heart expand in curiosity and openness to whatever is ready to meet you in this space
- Allow yourself to become totally saturated with your surroundings, remembering that everything you see, hear, and feel is a part of you

Mindful Cooking and Eating
- As you enter the kitchen to prepare food, take a moment to center yourself in the moment with a few deep breaths
- Give every moment of the cooking process your full attention, from washing, to cutting, to cooking. Become fully immersed in the process (you can do this even with simple meals, like mindfully spreading peanut butter on bread)
- Breathe loving-kindness into the cooking process, remembering that the food you make will provide nourishment to yourself and others
- Once the food is ready, clear the eating space of distractions. Avoid multi-tasking
- Chew every bite of food 20-30 times, letting yourself be engulfed in the flavor and practicing gratitude for the nourishment
- Walk away from your meal feeling truly nourished and renewed

Mindful Waiting
- The next time you're trying to distract yourself at the doctor's office, the mechanic, or waiting for a friend or colleague to arrive, remind yourself that waiting is one of the most sacred times to engage in mindfulness
- Breathe into the moment, becoming aware of what surrounds you
- Bring awareness to your body. How are you feeling? Take note of any sensations
- Become aware of the thoughts that come once you stop numbing yourself with distractions. What things are running through your mind?
- Pay attention to the deeper thoughts you may have previously been ignoring. Ask yourself what you can learn about yourself and your life, or if there are any actions you need to take.

Mindful Creativity (at least 5 minutes)
- Set aside anywhere from five minutes to several hours of undivided time
- Engage in a creative project like art, writing, dancing, etc.
- Bring full presence to the creative project and try to eliminate all expectations. Allow the moment to carry you.
- Pay attention to how your mind and body react as the moment carries you. How do you feel?
- Examine what you create as a result of this free-flowing creativity

Mindful Play

- Dedicate time each week to doing something truly fun—something that makes you feel like a kid again (climbing a tree, swimming in the lake, drawing with chalk, baking cookies, having a game night, etc.)
- Eliminate all distractions and allow this to be a moment to step away from your everyday life and responsibilities
- Allow yourself to become lost in the childlike joy of play. Laugh loudly, let your body dance, be curious.
- Let the feeling of childlike joy saturate your body and carry this joy with you as you move back into your daily life.

Mindful Movement (10-30 minutes)

- Choose one of your favorite forms of movement (swimming, walking, dancing, going to the gym, etc.) and dedicate at least ten minutes to it
- As you begin to move, establish a deeper sense of body awareness. Pay attention to the feelings in your body as you begin to warm up and exercise
- Pay attention to the way your heart beats, your lungs heave, your face begins to sweat, and your body tingles with the sense of being alive
- Thank your body for all it does for you.

Mindful Listening/Quality Time

- Apply this meditation to any quality time you spend with another person, whether that is grabbing coffee or going for a walk with a loved one, interacting with co-workers, are conversing with the grocery store cashier
- Before interacting with others, bring attention to your levels of empathy. Set the intention to hold space for other people and the moments you share with them
- Eliminate distractions (like technology) and allow yourself to put everything else going on in your life on pause in order to be fully present
- One of the best ways to show love for people and to cultivate personal mindfulness is through mindful listening. Focus all of your attention on the other person and what they are saying. When you ask how their day is going, be present to hear the answer.
- Do not think of what your next move will be, what you will say, or where you will go. Simply be there, showing loving-kindness, holding space, and taking it all in.

Mini Meditation Toolbox: 10 Quick and Easy Meditations to Ease Stress, Depression, Addiction, Anxiety, Pain, Distraction, and Loss Using Mindfulness

Journaling the Consciousness (10-minute meditation)

- Sit down with a journal and a pen and set your timer for 10 minutes
- As thoughts, worries, or emotions arise, immediately write them down. Do not worry about structure, grammar, or content, just write.
- When the time is up, look over what you wrote
- Ask yourself which themes seem to reoccur. Where are you feeling stress in your life? What is occupying most of your mental space?
- Close your eyes and take a few moments to breathe and meditate on the thing(s) that need your attention the most
- Open your eyes. Notice how you feel lighter and in touch with your experience

Distraction Cleanse: Clearing the Space in your Mind

- *Find a quiet place and begin to breathe*
- Ask yourself: "What is distracting me from being present right now?"
- Give space to that distraction, whether it is an invasive thought, personal emotion, or someone else's emotion

- Say to yourself: "I am letting my distractions move through me as I ground myself in the present moment. Nothing is more important than right now."
- Breathe until you feel the distraction melt away into presence and mental clarity.

Re-Writing the Moment: A Short Meditation to Ease Emotional Pain of the Past

- Sit down with a journal and a pen and set your timer for 1 minute
- Take this 1 minute to write down any moment(s) of the past which have caused you a lot of pain
- After the minute is up, choose one of the painful moments, close your eyes, and begin to imagine the moment in a safe way. Be sure to keep breathing.
- When you open your eyes, take your pen and paper and re-imagine the painful moment. What do you wish had happened? How do you wish you could think about the moment now?
- After re-imagining the painful moment, remind yourself that this is a new moment. Everyone has painful memories, but you do not have to stay in spaces of the past, which are painful for you.
- Close your eyes, take a few more breaths, and say to yourself, "I release the pain of that moment of the past. This is a new moment, and I will move with it."

Re-claiming your Inner Power: A Short Meditation to Face Addiction

- Breathe into the moment, allowing yourself to think about the implications your addiction has on your life
- Without judgment, question your addiction. Ask yourself, "What has been left empty in me that I am trying to fill with this?" Listen for any emotions or past experiences of trauma, grief, or abandonment that arise. Allow them to be there.
- Say to yourself, "Now that I understand the root of my addiction, I can begin to be set free."
- With closed eyes, begin to breathe. With each breath, imagine your addiction's hold on you weakening and weakening until eventually, you have been released.
- Move forward into your life with the idea that your addiction's hold on you is loosening, day by day.

Letter to the Lost: A Short Meditation to Address Grief and Loss

- Sit down with a journal and a pen and take five deep breaths to bring you into the moment
- Allow someone you have lost to come to mind. This can be a relationship that has ended, someone who has died, etc.
- Close your eyes and breathe into the space this person has left empty within you. Allow yourself to experience any emotions that arise.
- When you open your eyes, take a few minutes to write what you wish you could have said to that person

- After you have finished your letter, close your eyes again. Tell your grief that it is okay for it to be there. With every breath, imagine yourself moving forward in your life, released from every regret you may have with someone you've lost

In with The Positive, Out with the Negative: A Short Breathing Technique
- Find a comfortable space and prepare to use the 5-5-7 breathing technique
- Breathe in for five counts and think of something positive you want to bring into this moment (kindness, peace, wisdom, etc.)
- Hold for five counts, allowing this positive thing to fill your body
- Exhale for seven counts, thinking of something negative you want to release from your body in this moment (stress, tension, selfishness, etc.)
- Begin again with a second emotion. Do this as many times as you like until you feel well-equipped with positive emotions and have released all negative ones

Space to Breathe: A Short Meditation to Gain Control over your Anxiety
- When you begin to feel anxious, step away, take a breath, and ground yourself in the moment by finding one thing you can see, one thing you can hear, and one thing you can feel. Focus deeply on each thing.

- Allow your anxiety space to exist. Remember, anxiety is the reaction your emotional brain has when it senses a threat. You can bring yourself back from catastrophe mode by using the rational brain to repeatedly remind yourself: "I am safe. I am in control. I am capable of being calm."
- Keep breathing and saying these rational-brained affirmations until you begin to feel your anxiety melt away
- Move into the next moment feeling calm, anxiety-free, and empowered

Emotion Coding: A Short Meditation to Bring you in Touch with your Emotions

- Find a quiet, comfortable place where you can easily connect with yourself
- Close your eyes and breathe deeply (you may use a breathing pattern if desired)
- Begin to travel inwards. Say to yourself, "I am ready to accept the emotions that are here."
- Wait patiently, focusing on the breath, and observing every emotion that rises to the surface.
- When an emotion arises, ask yourself a series of questions:

    1. "Is this emotion mine or someone else's?"
    2. "Does this emotion serve me or hold me back?"
    3. "What is this emotion trying to teach me?"
    4. "Should I release this emotion or put it into action?"

- When it comes to answering each question, listen to your intuition. The answers to each question are already within you. Do not question your natural answers.
- If you are being told to release an old or negative emotion, or an emotion that belongs to someone else, breathe and imagine it melting away with every exhale
- If you are being told to foster a positive emotion or a strong emotion that can create positive change in the world, sit with that, breathing, and being open to how that emotion can be useful.

The "I Love..." Gratitude Meditation (2-minute meditation)
- Find a private space, preferably one in front of a mirror
- Start a timer for 2 minutes
- For two minutes, speak out loud sentences of gratitude beginning with the words "I love…" ("I love my partner," "I love coffee," "I love my cat," "I love sunflowers," "I love my mom," "I love to dance," "I love that I am healthy,").
- Say as many things as you can, one after the other. Do not think too much, simply let the things you love flow from your lips
- When the timer goes off, look in the mirror and say "And I love you," to yourself
- Feel the magic of gratitude transforming your life, your self-confidence, and your ability to be mindful

The Mindful Manifestation: A Short Meditation to Manifest what you Want in Life

- Sit down with a journal and pen
- Begin to cultivate mindfulness by bringing attention to your breath and any sensations in your body
- Ask yourself the question: "What do I want most in life?"
- As the answers start to come, open your eyes and begin to write your desires with the words "I manifest…" in front of them ("I manifest empathy." "I manifest peace of mind." "I manifest protection." "I manifest safety." "I manifest love." "I manifest awareness." "I manifest wisdom." "I manifest pure joy.")
- With each manifestation, close your eyes, and say it to yourself at least three times. Feel this manifestation become a part of your reality.

PART IV

Chapter 1: Self-Care Is the Best Care

"It is so important to take time for yourself and find clarity. The most important relationship is the one you have with yourself."

-Diane Von Furstenberg

Self-care is any activity that we deliberately do to improve our own well-being, whether it is physical, emotional, mental, or spiritual. The importance of taking care of one's self cannot be denied, as even health care training focuses on making sure healthcare workers are caring for themselves. If you do not take care of yourself, eventually, every other aspect o your life will fall apart, including your ability to help others.

This is a very simple concept, yet it is highly overlooked in the grand scheme of things. People lack the tendency to look after themselves and put their needs before anyone else. Good self-care is essential to improving our mood and reducing our anxiety levels. It will do wonders for reducing exhaustion and burnout, which is very common in our fast-paced world. It will also lead to positive improvements in our relationships.

One thing to note is that self-care does not mean forcing ourselves to do something we don't like, no matter how enjoyable it is to other people. For example, if your friends are forcing you to go to a party you rather not attend, then giving in is not taking care of yourself. If you would rather stay in and watch a movie, then that's what you should do, and it will be better for your well-being.

How Does Self-Care Work

It is difficult to pinpoint exactly what self-care is, as it is personal for everybody. Some people love to pamper themselves by going to the spa, while others enjoy physical activities like hiking, biking, or swimming. Some individuals take up art or other hobbies, like writing or playing a musical instrument. These activities are all different but will have the same type of benefits for the individuals engaging in them.

The main factor to consider when engaging in self-care is to determine if you enjoy the activity in question. If not, then it's time to move on. Self-care is an active choice that you actually have to plan out. It is time you set aside for yourself to make sure all of your needs are met. If you use a planner of any sort, make sure to dedicate some space for your particular self-care activities. Also, let people who need to know about your plans so you can become more committed. Pay special attention to how you feel afterward. The objective of any self-care activity is to make yourself feel better. If this is not happening, then it's time to change the activity.

While self-care, as a whole, is individualized, there is a basic checklist to consider.

- Create a list of things you absolutely don't want to do during the self-care process. For instance, not checking emails, not answering the phone, avoiding activities you don't enjoy, or not going to specific gatherings, like a house party.

- Eat nutritious and healthy meals most of the time, while indulging once in a while.
- Get the proper amount of sleep according to your needs.
- Avoid too many negative things, like news or social media.
- Exercise regularly.
- Spend appropriate time with your loved ones. These are the people you genuinely enjoy and not forced relationships.
- Look for opportunities to enjoy yourself and laugh.
- Do at least one relaxing activity a day, like taking a bath, going for a walk, or cooking a meal.

Self-care is extremely important and should not be an anomaly in your life.

How Does Self-Care Improve Self-Esteem and Self-Confidence?

To bring everything full circle, self-care plays a major role in improving self-esteem and self-confidence. It is easy to see how taking care of yourself will also make you feel better about yourself overall. All of these are actually inter-related, and a lack of one showcases a lack of the other. While caring for yourself also improves your self-esteem and self-confidence, not having self-esteem or self-confidence also leads to a lack of self-care. Basically, you believe that you are not good enough to be taken care of.

People with high self-esteem and self-confidence value themselves as much as they value others, and have no issues with making sure they're taken care of. They realize that it does not make them selfish or inconsiderate to think in this manner. Even if other people try to make them feel that way, a self-confident person will just brush off the criticism. An important thing to note is that when you take care of yourself, it does not mean you don't care about other people. It simply means you have enough self-love to not place yourself on the backburner.

Many people work so hard to try and please everyone else. This is one of the telltale signs of low self-esteem. While they're busy worried about other peoples' needs, their own get neglected, which will wear them down over time. The more they're unable to please someone, the harder they will try. What people in this situation don't realize is that some people are impossible to please, and it is not their responsibility to please them. That is up to the individual.

Poor self-care will eventually lead to poor self-image. It is possible that a person already has this initially. Self-care includes taking care of your hygienic and grooming needs. If you don't take the time to make yourself look good, this will significantly impact the value you place on yourself. When you are t work, among your friends, or just walking around town, not feeling like you look good will ultimately make you feel like you don't belong anywhere. Your confidence levels will plummet due to this.

Your health is another aspect to consider. Poor self-care means bad sleeping habits, unhealthy diets, lack of exercise, and more self-destructive behaviors. Your poor health practices can result in chronic illnesses down the line, like heart disease or diabetes. Once again, diminished health will lead to reduced self-confidence and self-esteem. Ask yourself now if putting other people ahead of you is worth it? I've got some news for you. The people who demand the most from you are probably looking out for themselves first.

The less a person takes care of themselves, the more their self-esteem and self-confidence will decline. It turns into a vicious downward cycle. This is why it is important to focus on all of these areas equally. When you find yourself neglecting your own self-care practices, it is time to shift your direction and bring your attention back to your needs. Ignoring your needs will ultimately lead to your fall. We will discuss specific practices and techniques for improving self-care in the next chapter.

Chapter 2:

What Does Good Self-Care Look Like?

Good Self-Care Practices

The following are some ways that good self-care will look like. If you find yourself having these qualities, then you are on the right path.

Taking Responsibility for Your Happiness

When you engage in self-care, it is truly self-care. This means you only rely on yourself, and nobody else, to make sure your needs are met. You realize that your happiness is no one else's responsibility but your own. You alone have the ability to control your outcomes. As a result of this independence, you will develop the skills and attitude you need to care for your own physical, mental, emotional, and spiritual well-being.

You Become Assertive With Others

People often take assertiveness for rudeness. This is not true, but if people believe that standing firm for what you want is rude, then that's their problem. Once you reach a certain mindset where self-care is important to you, then you will be unapologetically assertive. This means you have the ability to say "no" with confidence and stand by it. "No" is a complete sentence, and people will realize that quickly when they hear it from you.

You Treat Yourself As You Would a Close Friend

It's interesting how we believe that other people deserve better treatment from us than we do ourselves. We have a tendency to put our best friends in front of us, no matter how detrimental it is to our lives. This behavior stops once we engage in proper self-care. At this point, you will treat yourself as good as, or even better, than you treat your most beloved friends.

You Are Not Afraid to Ask for What You Want

Once you learn to take care of yourself, you also see your value increase within your mind. This means having an understanding that your voice, opinion, and needs matter, just like anybody with high self-esteem and self-confidence, would. As a result, you will not be afraid to ask for what you want, even if you might not get it.

Your Life Is Set Around Your Own Values

Once you practice self-care, you learn to check in with yourself before making important decisions. You always make sure the choices you are about to make line up with your purpose and values. If they go against them, then it's not a path you choose. This goes for the career you choose, where you decide to live, and the relationships you maintain in your life.

While all of the traits are focused on self, but it will lead to better relationships with other people too. When you practice self-care, you are in a better state in every aspect of your being. This gives you the ability to take care of and help those you need you, as well. Self-care is not an option, but a necessity, and it must never be ignored. Taking care of yourself is not selfish, no matter what anybody tells you. If someone tries to make you feel guilty over this matter, then consider distancing or removing them from your life. You are not obligated to maintain relationships with people.

Chapter 3: Demanding Your Own Self-Care

We went over the importance of self-care, and now we will focus on making it a reality in your life. If you want self-care to occur, you must be willing to demand it. The world is full of people who expect you to be at there beck-and-call every moment of the day. Some of these individuals are those who are closest to us, like friends or family members. This can make it harder to make our demands heard, but there is no way around it. Taking care of yourself is not an idea you can budge on. It is extremely important. We will go over several ways to maintain your ability for self-care in your life and provide detailed action steps to help you progress in this area.

Setting Healthy Boundaries

One of the biggest obstacles to self-care is other people who surround you. These are the true selfish individuals, whether they realize it or not, who believe they can barge in on your life and deserve all of your attention. They will take advantage of you, and if you are not careful, they will completely gain control of your emotions, and even your life. For proper self-care to occur, you must set firm and healthy boundaries with people. The following are steps that need to become mainstays in your life.

Identify and Name Your Limits
You must understand what your emotional, physical, mental, and spiritual limits are. If you do not know, then you will never be able to set real boundaries with people. Determine what behaviors you can tolerate and accept, and then consider what makes you feel uncomfortable. Identifying and separating these traits will

help us determine our lines.

Stay Tuned Into Your Feelings

Two major emotions that are red flags that indicate a person is crossing a barrier are resentment or discomfort. Whenever you are having these feelings, it is important to determine why. Resentment generally comes from people taking advantage of us or feelings of being unappreciated. In this instance, we are likely pushing ourselves beyond our limits because we feel guilty. Guilt-trips is a weapon that many people use to get their way. It is important to recognize when someone is trying to make you feel guilty because they are way overstepping their boundaries. Resentment could also be due to someone imposing their own views or values onto us. When someone makes you feel uncomfortable, that is another indication of a boundary crossed. Stay in tune with both of these emotions.

Don't Be Afraid of Being Direct

With some people, setting boundaries is easy because they have a similar communication style. They can simply read your cues and back off when needed. For other individuals, a more direct approach is needed. Some people just don't get the hint that they've crossed a line. You must communicate to them in a firm way that they have crossed your limits, and you need some space. A respectful person will honor your wishes without hesitation. If they don't, then that's on them. Your personal space is more important than their feelings.

Give Yourself Permission to Set Boundaries

The potential downfalls to personal limits are fear, self-doubt, and guilt. We may fear the other person's response when we set strong boundaries. Also, we may feel guilty if they become emotional about it. We may even have self-doubt on whether we can maintain these limits in the long run. Many individuals have the mindset that in order to be a good daughter, son, parent, or friend, etc., we have to say "yes" all the time. They often wonder if they deserve to have boundaries and limits with those closest to them. The answer is, yes, you do. You need to give yourself permission to set limits with people because they are essential to maintaining healthy relationships too. Boundaries are also a sign of self-respect. Never feel bad for respecting yourself.

Consider Your Past and Present

Determine what roles you have played throughout your life in the various relationships you have had. Were you the one who was always the caretaker? If so, then your natural tendency may be to put others before yourself. Also, think about your relationships now. Are you the one always taking care of things, or is it a reciprocal relationship? For example, are you always the one making plans, buying gifts, having dinner parties, and being responsible for all of the important aspects of the relationships? If this is the case, then tuning into your needs is especially important here. If you are okay with the dynamics of the relationship, then that's fine. I can't tell you how to feel. However, if you feel anger and resentment over this, then it's time to let your feeling be known, unapologetically.

Be Assertive

Once again, this does not mean being rude, even though some people will interpret it that way. Being assertive simply means being firm, which is important when reminding someone about your boundaries. Creating boundaries alone is not enough. You also have to stand by them and let people know immediately if they've crossed them. Let the person know in a respectful but strong tone that you are uncomfortable with where they're going, and they need to give you some space. Assertive communication is a necessity.

Start Small

Setting boundaries is a skill that takes a while to develop, especially if it's something you've never done before. Therefore, start with a small boundary, like no phone calls after a certain time at night. Make sure to follow through;

otherwise, the boundary is worthless. From here, make larger boundaries based on your comfort level.

Eliminating Toxicity and Not Caring About Losing Friends

If you plan on making self-care a priority in your life, I think that's great, and so should you. However, some people will have a problem with this. People don't always like it when their friends, family members, or acquaintances, etc., put themselves at the forefront of their lives. Once again, that is their problem, not yours. What is your problem, though, is distancing or even eliminating these individuals from your life. We will go over that in this section because part of self-care is eliminating toxicity from your life and not feeling bad about it.

Don't Expect People to Change

While everyone deserves a chance to redeem themselves, there comes the point where we must accept that people cannot change by force. They have to find it within themselves to make this change, and it is not our responsibility to do so. You may yearn to be the one who changes them, but it's usually a hopeless project. Toxic individuals are motivated by their problems. They use them to get the attention they need. Stop being the one to give it to them.

Establish and Maintain Boundaries

I already went in-depth on this, so I won't revisit it too much here. Just know that toxic people will push you to work harder and harder for them, while you completely ignore your own needs. This is exhausting and unacceptable. Create the boundaries you need with these individuals based on your own limits.

Don't Keep Falling for Crisis Situations

Toxic people will make you feel like they need you always because they are constantly in a crisis situation of some sort. It is a neverending cycle. When a person is in a perpetual crisis, it is of their own doing. They often create drama purposely to get extra attention. You may feel guilty for ignoring them, but remember that their being manipulative and not totally genuine.

I am not saying that you can't ever help someone who is going through a hard time. Of course, you can. Just don't start believing that you're responsible for their success or failure.

Focus on the Solution

Toxic individuals will give you a lot to be angry and sad about. If you focus on this, then you will just become miserable. You must focus on the solution, which, in this case, is removing drama and toxicity from your life. Recognize the fact that you will have less emotional stress once you remove this person from your life. If you let them, they will suck away all of your energy.

Accept Your Own Difficulties and Weaknesses

A toxic person will know how to exploit your weaknesses and use them against you. For example, if you are easy to guilt-trip, they will have you feel guilty every time you pull away from them. If you get to know yourself better and recognize these weaknesses, then you can better manage them and protect yourself. This goes along with creating self-awareness, which we discussed in chapter two. When you accept your weaknesses, you can work on fixing them and balance them with your strengths.

They Won't Go Easily

Recognize that a toxic individual may resist being removed from your life. Actually, if they don't resist, I will be pleasantly surprised. They may throw tantrums, but this is because they can't control or manipulate you anymore. They will even increase their previous tactics with more intensity. It is a trap, and you must not fall for it. Stay firm in your desire to leave and keep pushing forward. If they suck you back in, good luck trying to get out again.

Choose Your Battles Carefully

Fighting with a toxic person is exhausting and usually not worth it. You do not need to engage in every battle with them. They are just trying to instigate you.

Surround Yourself With Healthy relationships

Once you have removed a toxic person, or persons, from your life, then avoid falling into the trap with someone else. Fill your circle with happy and healthy relationships, so there is no room for any toxicity. Always remember the signs of a toxic person, so you can avoid them wholeheartedly in the future.

How to Focus on Self-Care

Now that we have worked to set boundaries and eliminate toxic people from our lives, it is time to focus on ourselves and the self-care we provide. The following are some self-care tips, according to psychologist, Dr. Tchiki Davis, Ph.D.

Pay Attention to Your Sleep

Sleep is an essential part of taking care of yourself. You must make it part of your routine because it will play a huge role in your emotional and physical well-being. There are many things that can wreak havoc on your sleep patterns, like stress, poor diet, watching television, or looking at your phone as you're trying to fall asleep. Think about your night routine. Are you eating right before bed or taking in a lot of sugar and caffeine? Are you working nonstop right up until bedtime? Have you given yourself some time to wind down before going to sleep? All of these factors are important to consider, as they will affect your sleep patterns. If you can, put away any phones, tablets, and turn off the television at least 30 minutes before you plan on going to bed.

Take Care of Your Gut

We often neglect our digestive tract, but it plays a major role in our health and overall well-being. When our gut is not working well, it makes us feel sluggish, bloated, and nonproductive. Pay attention to the food you eat as it will determine the health of your gut. It is best to avoid food with excess salt, sugar, cholesterol, or unhealthy fats. Stick to foods that are high in fiber, protein, healthy fats, and complex carbs. Some good options are whole grains, nuts, lean meats, fruits and vegetables, beans, and fish.

Exercise and Physical Activity Is Essential

Regular exercise is great for both physical and mental health. The physical benefits are obvious. However, many people do not realize that exercise will help the body release certain hormones like endorphins and serotonin. These are often called feel-good hormones because they play a major role in affecting our mood in a positive way. The release of these hormones will give us energy too, which will make us want to exercise more. Once exercise becomes a habit, it will be hard to break. Decide for yourself what your exercise routine will be, whether it's going to the gym, walking around the neighborhood, or playing a game of tennis.

Consider a Mediterranean Diet

While this is not a dietary book, the Mediterranean diet is considered the healthiest diet in the world because of its extreme health benefits. The food groups and ingredients that are used will increase energy, brain function, and has amazing benefits like heart and digestive tract health. The food also does not lack flavor, which shatters the myth that healthy food does not taste good.

Take a Self-Care Trip

Even if you are not much of a traveler, getting away once in a while can do wonders for your mental health. So often, our environment will make us feel stressed out, and it's good to remove ourselves from it for a couple of days. You do not have to take a trip abroad here. Of course, that is certainly an option. A simple weekend trip is perfectly fine. Just get yourself out of your normal routine and be by yourself for a while.

Get Outside

Nature and sunlight can be great medicines. It can help you reduce stress or worry, and has many great health benefits. Doing some physical activity outside, like hiking or gardening, are also great options.

Bring a Pet Into Your Life

Pets can bring you a lot of joy, and the responsibility they come with can boost your self-confidence by having to care for another living creature. Dogs are especially great at helping to reduce stress and anxiety. Animal therapy has been used to help people suffering from disorders lie PTSD, as well.

Get Yourself Organized

Organizing your life and doing some decluttering can do wonders for your mental and emotional health. Decide what area of your life needs to be organized. Do you need to clear your desk, clean out the fridge, or declutter your closet? Do you need to get a calendar or planner and schedule your life better? Whatever you can do to get yourself more organized, do it. Being organized allows you to know how to take better care of yourself.

Cook Yourself Meals At Home

People often neglect the benefits of a good home-cooked meal. They opt, instead, for fast-food or microwave dinners. These types of meals will make you full but will lack in essential nutrients that your body needs. Cooking nutritious meals at home will allow you to use the correct ingredients, so you can feel full and satisfied. Cooking alone can also be great therapy for people.

Read Regularly

Self-help books are a great read. However, do not limit yourself to these. You can also read books on subjects that you find fascinating or books that simply provide entertainment.

Schedule Your Self-Care Time

Just like you would write down an appointment time in your planner, also block out specific times for self-care activities. Stick to this schedule religiously, unless a true emergency comes up. This means that if a friend calls you to go out, you should respectfully decline their request and focus on yourself.

Chapter 4: How to Be Happy Being Alone

The final section of this book will focus on being alone and how to be happy about it. When you start engaging in self-care, you will also be spending much more time by yourself. A lot of people have a hard time dealing with this concept, especially if they're used to being around people all the time. However, for proper self-care, you have to be okay with being alone once in a while.

Accept Some Alone Time

The following are some tips to help you become happy with being alone. Soon, you will realize that your own company is the best kind.

Do Not Compare Yourself to Others
We are referring to your social life here. Do not compare to others, and do not feel like you must live as others do. If you do this, you may become jealous of a person's social circle or lifestyle. It is better to focus on yourself and what makes you happy. If you plan on spending significant time alone, then you cannot pay attention to what other people are doing.

Step Away From Social Media
If strolling through your social media page makes you feel left out, then take a step back and put it away for a while. During self-care moments, you are the focus, not what is happening with others online. Also, what people post on their pages is not always true. Many individuals have been known to exaggerate, or even flat-out lie on social media platforms. You may be feeling jealous or left out for no reason. Try banning yourself from social media for 24-48 hours, and see

how it makes you feel.

Take a Break From Your Phone

Avoid making or receiving calls. Let the important people in your life know that you will be away from your phone for a while, so they don't worry. When you are alone, really try to be alone.

Allow Time for Your Mind to Wander

If you feel unusual about doing nothing, it is probably because you have not allowed yourself to be in this position for a while. Carve out a small amount of time where you stay away from TV, music, the internet, and even books. Use this time to just sit quietly with your thoughts. Find a comfortable spot to sit or lie down, then just let your mind wander and see where it takes you. This may seem strange the first time, but with practice, you will get used to the new freedom.

Take Yourself on a Date

You don't need to be with someone else to enjoy a night out on the town. Take a self-date and enjoy your own company for a while. Go to a movie by yourself, stop by a nice restaurant, or just go do an activity you enjoy. If you are not used to hanging out alone, give it some time and you will become more comfortable with it. Take yourself on that solo date.

Exercise

We have mentioned exercise and physical activity a lot, but that's because it has so many great benefits related to self-care. Exercising will uplift your mood, and make it more enjoyable to be by yourself. Those feel-good hormones will provide a lot of benefits during these times.

Take Advantage of the Perks of Being Alone

Some people have spent so much time with other people that they've forgotten the perks of being alone. There are many to consider. First of all, you do not have to ask anyone's permission to do anything; you will have more personal space, can enjoy the activities you want to do, and don't have to worry about upsetting anyone. If you want, you can even have a solo dance party in your living room, Tom Cruise style. There are many advantages to being alone, so use them.

Find a Creative Outlet

It is beneficial to use some of your alone time to work on something creative. This can be painting, sculpting, music, writing, or any other creative endeavors. In fact, you can get out the watercolors and start fingerpainting. Creativity will bring a lot of joy into your life. It will make you happier about being alone.

Take Time to Self-Reflect

Being alone will give you the opportunity to self-reflect on your life. You won't care so much about being alone when you are coming up with important answers to your life.

Make Plans for Your Future

Planning out your life for five or ten years down the line will give you something important to do, and something to look forward to. Alone time is the perfect opportunity to determine these plans.

Make Plans for Solo Outings

Plan your solo outings based on what you like to do, whether it's a farmer's market, hiking, riding your bike, or going camping alone. Mak plans that will excite you, and you will be taking care of yourself while also being okay alone.

There are numerous topics that we went over in this chapter, but they all relate back to one theme: Self-care. Always remember that to take proper care of yourself, you must consider the following ideas:

- Setting Boundaries
- Avoiding and ridding yourself of toxic people
- Focus on yourself and your needs
- Be okay with being alone

Focus on these areas, and you will be demanding your own self-care without ever apologizing for it.

PART V

Chapter 1: Self-Esteem and Valuing Yourself

Imagine waking up in the morning and being full of life. You are energetic as you get out of bed and are ready to attack the day because nothing can stop you. Any type of challenge that comes your way, you are prepared to face it head-on and overcome it. You take pride in your work and relationships because you understand their worth. You also understand the value that you bring to the day, so you carry yourself with strength and dignity.

On the other hand, picture yourself waking up in a crummy mood. You are not looking forward to the day ahead, and no matter what good things may come, they are quickly tossed aside, and your mind wanders towards the negative side. You suffer from anxiety throughout the day, and you avoid any challenging situation you can because you lack faith in yourself.

These two mindsets are entirely different from one another, but they are related to the same thing: Your self-esteem. Self-esteem is the amount of respect that you place on yourself. It is how much you value your skills and ability to handle life and all its circumstances. Those who place a high value on themselves have a high level of self-esteem. Those who set a low value on themselves suffer from low self-esteem.

Your self-esteem is also your self-worth, and you mustn't put a low price tag on your abilities.

Having high self-esteem does not mean you ignore your flaws. It means that you love yourself despite all of them. You recognize your weaknesses, and therefore, are more likely to fix them. In the end, you love yourself because of your own self-beliefs.

As we grow up, we are constantly surrounded by things that affect our psyche. Our ego is the part of our mind that has a direct relationship with the outside world. When we experience an event or interact with a specific individual, it will determine how we feel at that exact moment. If the situation is upsetting, then it can bring out a range of different emotions in us. For those who are dealing with low self-esteem, they will easily be triggered by an outside event. For example, if someone calls us a negative name, it might make us feel sad or angry. This one incident could ruin our whole day in an instant. If we are experiencing negativity over a long period of time, then these thoughts will slowly enter into our subconscious and unconscious mind, where they stay forever, unless we purposefully remove them.

If you have a healthy level of self-esteem, then these situations will roll off your back. Negative people or situations will not change the feelings you have towards yourself because you will be in complete control of your emotions. I am not suggesting that being insulted will not be hurtful for this type of individual, but they will understand how to manage it and not let it affect them negatively. They don't define themselves by other people's opinions.

I can talk all day about the extreme benefits of self-esteem, as there are many. The focus of this book, though, is how to develop and build your self-esteem, even if you have been suffering from low levels of it your whole life. I am working off the assumption that you are in the camp of low self-esteem. Therefore, you already know how it feels, because you are personally living it.

How Low Self-Esteem Is Developed

The first step in dealing with low self-esteem is recognizing that you have it. Now that we have established that, it is important to determine why you have low self-esteem.

The Different Types of Parents

One of the major contributing factors to our self-esteem is our parents and how they raised us. Our mother and father are generally the first people we become close to. How they interact with us will initially determine how we value ourselves. Even if a parent is loving, there are still specific tendencies that can be counterproductive to use raising our self-worth.

While parents often push their children to succeed, some can become overbearing to the point where they use ridicule, harsh criticisms, and even abuse to ensure their children stay on the straight path. While some parents do not have malicious intent when they become disapproving authority figures, others will purposefully look down on their kids and make them feel inferior. Children who grow up under these conditions grow into adults who are never comfortable in their own skin.

On the opposite end of the overbearing caregiver is the uninvolved caregiver who does not care one bit. They ignore their children as if they are not necessary. In fairness, this can often be done unintentionally. For example, the parents work so much and become excessively focused on their jobs. They are obsessed with making a living and ignore the people closest to them, including their children. When children get ignored by the influential adults in their lives, they become confused about their place in the world. They feel forgotten and unimportant, and therefore, they believe their existence to be bothersome to people.

Another parental issue that affects children is the parents or caregivers who are in constant conflict. When these adults fight and throw hurtful language at one another, especially in front of children, they absorb these negative emotions. These children can feel like they contributed to the fighting in some way. Growing into adulthood, these same children will feel like they are the cause of so many different conflicts, simply because they were nearby.

Bullying

Bullying has been an issue for children and adults alike for generations. The powerful always seem to push around the weak. With children, this power is usually in the form of physical dominance. The bigger and stronger child picks on the smaller and weaker one. Of course, the bullying can be mental or psychological, too, if the child can pull it off.

Bullying can also become a significant contributor to low self-esteem. A child who is constantly bullied in any way will develop a poor self-image about themselves. Unfortunately, bullying will never go away. What matters in these situations is the support that children receive from their parents. The way the adults in a child's life handle the aftermath of bullying will play a major role in their mindset development.

Many children do not have a comforting environment to come home to, which is detrimental to their psyche. After experiencing abuse outside the come, they walk through their front door and experience even more of it. This makes a child feel worthless and abandoned. They become lost further into the abyss and think they do not belong anywhere. Having unsupportive parents will magnify the effects of bullying.

Furthermore, some parents were over-supportive. These are the ones who coddled their children and gave them no coping skills to deal with the outside world. As a result, they will be ill-prepared to deal with the cruel world that exists out there, which is not going away anytime soon. When children become adults and enter the real world, they will face some harsh criticisms that will challenge their beliefs about who they are. If they were always buttered up as children, they would not understand how to face rejection, insults, or people being mean to them.

No parent wants their children to feel bad, but they cannot be shielded from disappointment their whole lives. Once they do face this disappointment in the real world, they will fall apart because they have no actual self-worth. All of their value is tied to the compliments that other people give them.

I know I have been singling out parents here, and that's because they are the adults a child spends the most amount of time with. However, other adults, like extended family members, teachers, coaches, or counselors, can also do their part in providing a supportive atmosphere for the children in their lives.

Trauma

Trauma can be physical, emotional, or sexual, and no matter what kind you were a victim of, it will devastate your self-esteem, especially as a child. With trauma, you are being forced into a position against your will, which makes you feel like you've lost power and control of your situation.

Situations like this will make you feel worthless. You will even blame yourself for causing the trauma or abuse. This is a method many people use to gain control back into their lives. They believe that by taking the blame, they will be able to manage the situation the next time it comes around

Children do not have control over who is in their lives. This means they are often stuck in abusive situations and have no way of getting out of it. If they are lucky, someone will recognize it, and they will help them get out.

A child who goes through trauma will grow into an adult who is unsure of themselves in many ways. They will never feel like they are good enough, will always feel like they are to blame for specific situations, and will have a distrust for humanity in general.

I know I have spoken about a lack of trust throughout this book. A significant part of having self-esteem is being able to put your faith into the unknown. When you lack trust, this faith does not exist, and therefore, you will always be paranoid and never fully confident in any situation.

Now, think back on your life and determine the traumatic events you may have gone through. How did these affect your psyche at that moment? How you felt on the inside when these various circumstances occurred will help you understand if they contributed to a lack of self-esteem.

We went over these issues simply to help you recognize the underlying causes of the value you place on yourself. There is nothing we can do about these situations now, but we can learn from them and work on ways to overcome our mental blocks to positive self-esteem.

The Science of Self-Esteem

There has been a lot of research done on the genetic components of low self-esteem. While people can be born with certain levels of chemicals that influence their emotions and brain activity, there is no conclusive evidence that people are born with high or low self-esteem. Even twins who grew up in different environments were found to have different qualities related to their self-worth, even though various other personality traits were similar. As of now, environmental factors seem to play a much more significant role.

Of course, this does not mean that there is no scientific component to all of this. As we go through various life stages, our brain development occurs based on life experiences. The actions we take and the thoughts we create make numerous neural pathways in our brain and nervous system, which determine our future behavior. For example, if we continuously have negative feelings, our mind becomes wired in a certain way to produce these same thoughts in the future. As a result, you habitually think negatively in every situation you come across.

Now that we have established what low self-esteem is, our goal in the next chapter is to help you rewire your brain, so you can start living with high self-esteem.

Chapter 2: How You Can Matter to Yourself

"Confront the dark parts of yourself, and work to banish them with illumination and forgiveness. Your willingness to wrestle with your demons will cause your angels to sing."

-August Summer

Now that we know what self-esteem is, it is hard to deny the role it plays in our lives. Any type of pursuit, whether personal, professional, relationships, or health, will require you to place a high value on yourself; otherwise, you will never progress forward as you should. At this moment, I want you to recognize the past mistakes that brought you to where you are now, but also forgive yourself for them because you can do nothing to change the past. You can learn from it, though, and build a new future where you actually value yourself and the gifts you bring to the world.

In the previous chapter, we discussed the numerous causes of low self-esteem, many of which stem from our childhood. Since our mindset took a long time to develop, it will take extreme effort with several actionable steps to change and overcome this thought-process. We will now discuss some specific steps and practices over the next few chapters you can engage in to improve your mindset and build-up your self-esteem.

We will approach this subject from many different aspects, so they can be combined to improve how you habitually think about yourself. Think of your mind as a structure that is built to think a specific way. Now imagine having to rebuild many different parts of that structure to change your thoughts. This is what we will be doing with all of the action steps we will go over.

How to Build Self-Awareness

Self-awareness means having the ability to understand the way you think, feel, and behave. This is a necessary quality to have if you want to fix your self-esteem. It is the best way to recognize if your actions correlate with low self-esteem. Once you become self-aware, you will know yourself much better. The following are some significant strategies you can employ right away.

Recognize What Bothers You About Other People

What bothers us most about other people are often the same qualities that we possess. For example, if someone is naturally aggressive, we may dislike it; however, it is a trait that we have, as well. We all have aspects of our personality that are unflattering, and since we don't want to admit them, we will ignore them fully. Ignorance is not bliss in the long-run, and if we do not pay attention to our negative qualities, they will rear their ugly heads at the most inopportune time. The next time a person is bothering you, stop and ask yourself if they are displaying something that is a reflection of you. Do you recognize their personality when you look in the mirror?

Meditate on Your Mind

Mindful meditation is a great way to learn about your thoughts and how they work. One of the main reasons we lack self-awareness is because we are thinking so much that our thoughts completely take over. Proper meditation allows us to separate ourselves from these thoughts and recognize that they do not fully encompass who we are. Through mindful meditation practices, you have the ability to observe your thoughts without becoming attached to them. Therefore, it is easier to see which ones deserve our attention and which ones do not. The following are some simple steps to get you started on this practice.

- Get comfortable by finding a quiet place that is as free from distractions as possible.
- Sit up with your back straight and chest out. It does not matter if you are in a chair or sitting cross-legged on the floor. You may even lie down flat on the floor.
- Take in some deep breaths through your nose and then out slowly through your mouth or nose. You should be able to feel the breaths down into your abdomen. This will help you relax.
- Pay attention to the sounds of your breaths and their rhythmic patterns. When you inhale, imagine breathing in joy and peace. When you breathe out, imagine getting rid of the toxicity in your mind.
- When you notice your thoughts wandering away from your breaths, immediately focus them back to the center. Take in your

immediate surroundings and be in your present state. Do not think of the past or worry about the future.

- Make this practice a habit and do it routinely. Some of the best practitioners of mindful meditation have been doing it for years, and are still learning better ways to improve. These are all great steps to get you started and reorganize your mind.

As a side note, meditation is not only useful for self-awareness. It can help with stress and anxiety, communication, better sleep, improved focus on your goals, and overall mental health. All of this will lead back to higher self-esteem. Start off with five minutes and then build yourself up to 20-30. You will be amazed at how much clarity you will have about yourself.

Draw a Timeline of Your Life

Sit down with a notepad and try to remember as much as you can from the time of birth to where you are now. Pay special attention to significant moments that had a big impact on your life and circumstances, whether positive or negative. This practice will allow you to see certain moments of your life in context, which will give you a better idea of who you are. You will realize a lot about yourself and gain much self-awareness.

Identify Your Emotional Kryptonite

Think about the emotions that you absolutely hate having and try to avoid. For example, some individuals hate feeling sad so much that they drown this emotion with alcohol. The problem is, negative emotions are a gateway into our souls. They are trying to tell us something in a discrete way. If we pay attention to them as they are happening, we will learn a lot about our situation. If you are sad often, pay attention to why so you can finally address it.

Travel and Get Out a Little Bit

We often become stuck in our own little box and forget that there is a big world out there. Micro-travel, which means traveling to new destinations that are local to us, is a great way to get you out of your comfort zone and try out a new routine. Take frequent short trips if you can, and even travel abroad if this is feasible. This will help you gain a lot of awareness for the world around you, as well as teach you a lot about yourself. Travel to new destinations, even nearby, will significantly raise our self-awareness.

Pick Up a New Skill

Just like with travel, learning a new skill will force us to think and act in new ways, thereby forcing us to increase our self-awareness. We all develop certain routines as we grow older, and it causes us to go into a comfort zone. The main problem here is that it creates a strong, narrow-mindedness. Being willing to start something as a beginner will cultivate a level of flexibility in our minds and thoughts. The new skill does not have to be related to your career. It can also be hobbies like playing the piano, sculpting, or dancing.

Clarify Your True Values

How often do you sit down and assess what your true values are? If you are like most people, probably very seldomly. We often get so caught up in daily life that we have very little time for self-reflection, especially on the important things in life. As a result, we end up chasing false goals and not living the type of life we want to. People become so worried about moving up the career ladder and buying the latest fancy car, that they forget what actually makes them happy. In your case, you may have followed a safe career path rather than focus on what your true calling was.

A great technique you can perform is to set aside some time on a weekly or monthly basis and think about your life and circumstances. Ask yourself why you think you are here and what your purpose in life is? Also, imagine what a fulfilling life would look like for you. Spend about 30 minutes every time you do this. A major part of self-awareness is recognizing what really matters to you. This practice will be a great way to come to this understanding.

We tend to get lost in the monotony of life. So, it is important to practice these self-awareness techniques on a regular basis. Taking notice of your thoughts, behaviors, and actions in real-time is a special skill to have. It will go a long way in helping you build your self-esteem.

Chapter 3: Creating a Stronger Self

Going along the path of improved self-esteem, I will now discuss various strategies to strengthen your psyche. High self-esteem requires a strong mindset.

Managing Your Ego

I spoke briefly in chapter one about the ego. Our ego is basically our mind's direct connection to the outside world. What our environment gives, our ego responds. This means that whatever activities are going on around will make you feel a certain way, and this is directly the result based on how our ego responds. For example, if someone outshines us in some way, our ego will respond by making us feel inferior.

People who are not careful will have this aspect of the mind completely control them. As a result, the values they place on themselves are based on what the world thinks of them, rather than what they think of themselves. Every one of us has an ego to a certain degree, but the key is to not let it control us. We must learn to manage it properly so that our self-worth comes from within, rather than from what we can't control. The following are specific steps you can take to begin managing your ego so that it doesn't control you.

Don't Take Things Personally

Taking things too personally or literally can make you overthink and cause your mind to become infected. It's important to be at peace with yourself and realize that people do not always mean what they say. They are often angry or suffering from some other negative emotion. Even if they do mean it, people who treat others poorly have a problem within themselves, and not necessarily other people. In a moment where you are facing harsh words or actions, imagine your spot being replaced by someone else and watching the same people act in the same manner because, in most cases, they would. A big part of self-esteem is not caring what others think. This is a major step in that direction.

Accepts All of Your Mistakes

Accepting your mistakes, no matter how big or small is a positive way to work on your ego problems. Everyone makes mistakes, so there is no use in hiding them. Once you admit them, apologize, and move on, they no longer have control over you as you've released them from your psyche. Genuinely apologizing to someone is a great way to put your ego in check and grow as a person.

Stop Being Self-Conscious

Our ego prevents us from looking silly or goofy. We are so afraid of what others are thinking that we never let out guard down. This is a real definition of living in fear. If you have been acting this way for a while, then it's time to stop putting up a shield, and just let your silly self come out. You will actually be happier in the long run because showcasing your true self will attract your real friends. To stop being so self-conscious, try using the following steps.

- Shrug away your negative thoughts. This does not mean you should ignore them. Acknowledge that they are there, but then do not agree with them in any way.

- Don't put other people on pedestals. We have a tendency to do this, especially to those who we admire. Realize that they are regular people and not someone to bow down to.

- Think of a moment where you were self-conscious, and then imagine replacing yourself with someone you cared about in the position. If they felt the same way you did, then what would you tell them. Now, tell that same thing to yourself. We are often bigger critics of ourselves than we are other people.

- Accept yourself, with your faults and all. Remember that nobody is perfect, and if you want to gain a high level of self-esteem, then you must learn to love yourself, including your flaws.

- People are not paying as much attention to you as you may think. Part of our ego tells us that people are watching us and critiquing our every move. Understand that people are in their own world much of the time, and too busy in their personal self-doubts to pay attention to anyone else. Believe it or not, you are not the focus of attention all the time.

- Go do the thing that makes you self-conscious or nervous. Face it head-on, and you will realize it's not as bad as you may think. Do not let your awkwardness keep you on the sidelines. Jump in with both feet and dare to look foolish. If you hate dancing in front of people, join a dance class and do it several times a week. If you suck at basketball, go to the part and shoot hoops in front of people.

Realize That Your Ego Will Never Go Away

Controlling and managing your ego will have to become a routine in your life. It will never fully go away and will rear its ugly head at the most inopportune times if you let your guard down. Always be on high alert of your ego trying to take over, and you will continue to overcome it.

You Are Not the Best

I am not trying to be insulting here, but knowing that you are not going to be the best in every situation means that you understand your limitations. Everyone has limitations, so there is no sense in feeling bad over them. Accept that you are not perfect, but recognize that it does mean you cannot accomplish your goals. You may just need to work harder and focus more on certain areas.

Imagine Your Ego as Another Person

This step may seem ridiculous, but imagine your ego as another person. It is best to picture someone that you may listen, but never actually take advice from, like a whining child. Now, once you imagine your ego in this manner, allow it to speak and say what it needs, acknowledge it with a "thank you," and then move on. When you can actually picture your ego in this way, it will do a lot in stopping you from making significant mistakes.

Stop Bragging

There is no need to brag about your accomplishments. If they are great enough, other people will do the talking for you. The less you talk about yourself, the more humble you become, and humility is a major aspect of self-esteem. You never feel the need to talk yourself up.

Be Grateful for the Little Things

Gratitude is great for improving your attitude. When you start being grateful for the little things, you do not worry so much about the big things. Also, remember that some people cannot have what you have, no matter how hard they try. With the same token, some people will be in a different position than you, that you are unable to reach. That is okay. Just focus on yourself and what you have.

Learn to Compliment Others

People with large egos have a hard time admitting when others have done a great job. They feel it will take the spotlight off of them. Practicing paying even the smallest compliments to other people can help you take the attention off of your ego problems.

On top of these practices, we have gone over, a few other ways to get rid of your ego include:

- Embrace a beginner's attitude. Try something new regularly that forces you to challenge yourself. This will help you realize that you are not perfect at everything.
- Concentrate on the effort you put in, and not the results. You will be forced to see how much you put into an activity, and determine if you did too much, or not enough.
- Never stop learning, even if it's not something you will ever use. It keeps you humble.
- Validate yourself once in a while.
- Never expect rewards or recognition. Do what is right, simply because it is the right thing to do.
- Do not try to control everything.

Forgiving People

Since so much of our self-esteem is tied up in what the people of our past did or did not do for us, it is important to forgive those who may have harmed us. We often hold onto grudges, and this prevents us from moving forward. Part of having self-esteem is no longer allowing others to control us. If the actions of people in the past still impact the opinion we have of ourselves, then we are still under there control. The main idea of forgiveness is that you have the ability to move on without having to carry a heavy burden any longer. Here is what forgiveness does not mean:

- Condoning harmful behavior.
- Accepting someone back into your life.
- Forgetting the incident or incidents that harmed you.
- Having to talk to the person again in any way.
- You are helping the other person. Of course, this may be a secondary benefit, which is fine.

By forgiving someone, you are accepting the reality that they did something terrible to you, but it no longer has to define you. Forgiveness is 100 percent for your own benefit.

The first step in forgiveness is the willingness to actually forgive someone. Just imagine that the anger you have for someone is a bag of rocks that you have been carrying on your back. After many years, this becomes very exhausting, both physically and mentally. Now, imagine that forgiveness means dropping that bag of rocks forever. You will feel much better when you put down the bag, and you will feel much better once you forgive. When you are ready, then utilize the following steps to help you get past, well, your past.

- Think about the particular incidents that angered you. Accept that they happened and what your feelings were when they did. In order to forgive, you must acknowledge what happened. You cannot just ignore it. This is why forgetting is not part of the process. For example, the incident could have been that your parents were absent and did not pay any attention to you.

- Acknowledge the growth in yourself that happened after the incident occurred. What did it make you learn about yourself and the world? For example, if your parents were absent for much of your life, perhaps it taught you how to be independent and survive on your own. That is a pretty big deal.

- Now think about the other person. The one that actually caused the incident. Realize that they were working from a limited frame of mind and did not have the benefit of hindsight. When they harmed you in some way, they were probably trying to have one of their needs met. Think about what that need may have been, and if it changes your perspective on them. In reference to your parents, maybe they were absent and did not pay attention to you because they were worried about always having food on the table and a roof over your head. This caused them to work incessantly, and when they were home, they were too tired to give you the right amount of attention. It's possible that they hated being absent just as much as you did.

- Finally, say the words, "I forgive you." It is up to you whether you want to tell the person or not. In any event, tell yourself.

Forgiveness will help you put closure on your past so that you can focus on moving forward. This is an important step forward to gaining self-esteem. You will no longer be bound by what happened to you in the past; therefore, you will be free.

Overcoming Trauma

Since trauma plays a major role in a person's self-image, it is important to identify the negative thoughts that will lead to low self-esteem. Once you catch these thoughts, then you can combat them head-on. You may never forget about the trauma, but just like the hurt you received from people of your past, you can keep it from controlling you. The following are a few simple steps you can take to help you improve your negative self-image related to trauma. These practices have been used widely with people suffering from Post Traumatic Stress Disorder.

- Identify your negative thoughts. Once negative thoughts become part of your routine, they can easily slip by without getting caught. Self-monitoring can be a great way of increasing awareness of your thoughts and how they are affecting your mood and behavior. You must do this consciously. You may also sit down at the end of each day and run down what you did. Think about all of the negative thoughts you had, what caused them, and how you reacted. This can also make you more aware of them in the future. We often have specific triggers that affect our mood.

- Once you learn to identify negative thoughts, slow them down. The more you think about negative thoughts, the more intense they become. Therefore, once you identify them, distract yourself by thinking of something else. This is not about avoidance, but taking a step back and reducing the intensity of these thoughts. Often times, we cannot deal with negativity because it becomes so overwhelming. Once we remove ourselves from the situation a little bit, then we can manage things more appropriately.

- After reducing the intensity of your thoughts, it is now time to challenge them. Many times, we accept our thoughts at face value without actually questioning them. As a result, we do not actually know why we are thinking negatively during a certain situation. We just know that we always have. Challenge your thoughts by asking some of the following questions:

    o What evidence is there for having these thoughts?
    o What evidence is there that are against these thoughts?
    o Are there moments when these thoughts have not been true?
    o Do I only have these thoughts when I am sad, angry, or depressed, or do I have them when I am feeling okay, as well?
    o What advice would I give someone else who is also having these thoughts?
    o Is there any type of alternate explanation?

- Counter your negative thoughts further by using positive self-supportive statements. For example, you can tell yourself all of your recent accomplishments, the good qualities you do possess, or positive things you are looking forward to in the future, like starting a new job or taking a vacation. Basically, counter negative thoughts with positive ones. It is beneficial to write some of these down so you can refer to them in the future. When you are drowning in negativity, it can be difficult to come up with positive statements about yourself.

- As a side note, you do not have to use positive self-supportive statements exclusively when you are upset. You can tell them to yourself any time to build up your positivity.

Chapter 4: Changing Our Minds

For the final chapter in this section, we can start focusing on shifting the mindest fully towards high self-esteem. Once this occurs, we must continue to follow the strategies I have gone over to never lose your self-esteem. If you let your guard down, it will happen.

How To Ignore Things

Our self-esteem continues to remain low throughout our lives because we always let things bother us. Many of these things are beyond our control, so we should not pay them any mind. The reason people achieve their lifelong goals is that they don't let their surroundings affect their minds. The following are some ways to ignore what bothers you, so you can keep moving forward while loving yourself.

Stop Comparing Yourself To Others

The bottom line is, you are not someone else, and they are not you. Just because someone else looks great in a dress or suit, does not mean you have to, as well. Also, understand that other people will not look as good as you in certain outfits. Some people will look great all dressed up, while others pull off the casual look better.

If you are not comfortable, then you will never feel right in any situation.

Therefore, do not force yourself into something, simply because other people are doing it. Understand yourself through self-awareness and focus on the things that make you feel good. You can't compare yourself to others, and they can't compare themselves to you. Work on impressing the person in the mirror and no one else.

Ignore Societal Pressure

Have you ever done something because someone you don't like or even know might become impressed, even though they don't actually care about you? If this statement sounds ridiculous, imagine actually living. Oh, wait! Many people are already. This is because they are under some sort of societal pressure to live a certain way, even though most people in society don't matter to them in the long run. To stop allowing this to happen, ask yourself the following questions.

- Who will be responsible after I kill my dreams to produce a fake image, society, or me?
- Are the people around me genuinely concerned about my happiness? If not, then why do I care so much?
- Will the people pressuring me even matter five years from now?
- Am I alone in feeling this societal pressure?

After answering all of these questions, you will realize that your situation is not unique. Many people are pressured by society and trying to hold up a fake image. This means they are not happy because they are not willing to share their true selves. Ultimately, you will be living your own existence, whether you choose it or someone else does.

Start Living In The Present Moment

So many people live in the past, and therefore, their old mistakes still have an impact on their present state of mind. It's time to get over your past. The following are some tips to help you do so.

- Create some physical distance between yourself and the person or situation that is reminding you of your past. This could mean cutting off some close people or physically moving somewhere else.
- Stay busy working and improving yourself, that you have no time to worry about what happened in the past.
- Treat yourself like you would a best friend. We tend to be gentler with others than ourselves.
- Don't shut out negative emotions. Let them flow through you so you can overcome them.
- Don't expect an apology from other people. Even if you were wronged by them, they might not think so. Therefore, move on and accept that they haven't come to terms with anything, but you have.
- Give yourself permission to talk about your pain, even if it's just to yourself. In any event, let it out. Let the past pain escape out of you.

Leverage Your Purpose

This will give your life more meaning. First, leverage your purpose to serve others. Help someone else realize their dreams through your own unique talents. There are many unique ways to do this, including teaching, coaching, and mentoring. Do this on a volunteer basis. Whatever gives purpose to your life, share it with someone else.

Try out these different practices and feel yourself start ignoring all of the noise around you. It is distracting, and you must be able to filter it.

The Mindset Shift

We have gone over many different aspects of the mind and how to change certain thought-processes. What happens with these techniques is a total mindset shift. Instead of your mind being wired to think negatively about everything, including yourself, you will now habitually think in a positive way and understand the values you bring to the world, which are a lot. The goal of all of the previous practices and strategies is to rewire your neural pathways to help change your mindset.

Your mindset was developed over a long period of time, which means the neural pathways you have are build up pretty strong. For this reason, they must be worked on regularly to help break them down and build new ones up. So, do not treat these techniques as a one-and-done cure. They must become a regular part of your lifestyle. Once they are, then you will be amazed at the results you have. When your self-esteem is high, you will:

- Have no problem being yourself.
- Be able to disagree without attacking someone.
- Not be swayed so easily by the opinions of others.
- Be able to articulate your views and be able to defend them appropriately when challenged.
- No longer fear uncertainty.
- Be much more resilient and tough.
- Never need approval from anyone to live your life as you choose.
- Value yourself and have high self-worth, despite what others may think of you.
- Not act like you know everything.
- Be okay with not being perfect.
- Never again let your past define who you are.

Once you go from low to high self-esteem, you will feel like a completely different person. You will still acknowledge your past pain, but it will not control you.

Now That Your Self-Esteem is High

After going through all of the practices, thoughts, and feelings inside of you will be different because you will have effectively restructured your mind. The plan now is to keep revisiting these techniques, so you never fall back into the abyss ever again. Now that your self-esteem is high, you will sense the following beliefs flowing through you.

- No matter what you've done, you are worthy of love. You understand your past mistakes, but will not degrade yourself over them.

- You are not defined by your "stuff." You will enjoy what you have, but your happiness will not be dependent on it.

- You will allow yourself to feel all of your emotions, and not be ashamed of them.

- You won't care if you miss out on things. You will feel okay about staying alone because your company is good enough.

- You will not be worried about what happens to you, because you will be able to respond appropriately, There will be challenges, but the end result will be in your favor.

- You will be doing what you love. You will look forward to every day.

- You will understand that people are judging you based on something within themselves.

- You will never think the world revolves around you. There is a higher power out there greater than anything that exists on Earth. This does not have to be a diety, but it certainly can be for you.

- You will find things to be grateful for every day. Because you are looking, you will find them.

www.ingramcontent.com/pod-product-compliance
Lightning Source LLC
Chambersburg PA
CBHW071629080526
44588CB00010B/1331